William Andrews, William Berry, William Harrison Ainsworth

History of the Dunmow Flitch of Bacon Custom

William Andrews, William Berry, William Harrison Ainsworth

History of the Dunmow Flitch of Bacon Custom

ISBN/EAN: 9783337326029

Printed in Europe, USA, Canada, Australia, Japan

Cover: Foto ©ninafisch / pixelio.de

More available books at **www.hansebooks.com**

HISTORY

OF THE

Dunmow Flitch of Bacon Custom,

BY

WILLIAM ANDREWS,

FELLOW OF THE ROYAL HISTORICAL SOCIETY.

POEMS

BY

WILLIAM HARRISON AINSWORTH.
WILLIAM BERRY.
J. J. BRIGGS, F.R.S.L.
Madame CLARA DE CHATELAIN.
LE CHEVALIER DE CHATELAIN.
Mrs. G. M. TWEDDELL.
GEORGE MARKHAM TWEDDELL.

Historical Notices of Ceremonies similar to that of Dunmow.

LONDON:
WILLIAM TEGG & CO., PANCRAS-LANE, CHEAPSIDE.
MDCCCLXXVII.

TO

WILLIAM HARRISON AINSWORTH, Esq.,

NOVELIST, POET, GENTLEMAN,

This little History of a good

𝕺𝖑𝖉 𝕰𝖓𝖌𝖑𝖎𝖘𝖍 𝕮𝖚𝖘𝖙𝖔𝖒,

Which he revived, is dedicated by

HIS OBEDIENT SERVANT,

W. A.

PREFACE.

We have written this little book because we are greatly interested in the good old Custom of Dunmow. The usage being curious, and so well calculated to promote domestic felicity, we deem it desirable to produce in a popular form a work on the subject. Grose says " Amongst the jocular tenures of England, none have been more talked about than the Bacon of Dunmow," yet, strange to relate, to the present time no history in a separate form has appeared, hence our wish to furnish one. We agree with the poet when he sings :—

> It were well if " our Custom " so widely was spread,
> That every fond couple resolv'd to be wed ;
> Would determine to please, to charm, and bewitch,
> That in *any year* they might each claim the Flitch.
>
> Should this be the case a glad world would be ours,
> The thorns and the briars would bloom into flowers;
> And all might rejoice, the poor and the rich,
> If all would *deserve* and lay claim to the Flitch.

We have done our best to render our work attractive not only to the antiquary, but to the general reader. In our labour of love we have received much kind assistance, and amongst those we must thank for favours in furnishing poetical contributions and historical information, W. Harrison Ainsworth, Esq., William Berry, Esq., Le Chevalier de Chatelain, S. F. Longstaffe, Esq., F.R.H.S., F. Ross, Esq., F.R.H.S., our very dear friends Mr. and Mrs. G. M. Tweddell, of Stokesley. Mr. John William Savill, of Dunmow, at considerable trouble, has enriched us with valuable notes that have been of the greatest service in compiling this work. It is only right to state the promoters of the Dunmow Custom have in Mr. Savill a most energetic secretary and manager.

He is a gentleman of literary ability and has a taste for archæology. Several newspapers of the county have in him a good representative. He is a contributor to a number of our magazines, where his articles are always instructive and interesting, and receive a good share of attention, being free from political and religious bias, though at times keen and sarcastic. In 1863 he produced his "History of Dunmow," which contains much valuable information conveyed in a clear and pleasing manner. It was favourably noticed by the critical press, and merited the reception it obtained from the general public. Topographers would do well to take as a model the arrangement of this work. The large edition was rapidly exhausted and the work is now unattainable. "The Dunmow Almanac" was year by year brought out by Mr. Savill with great taste, for a period of seven years. He also published "How to make Home Happy"—a work containing golden rules which, if followed, would result in rendering the family circle a nearer type to the heavenly one than it often is. "The Family Doctor," an elaborate book of Hygeine, followed, and some thousands are in circulation. Copies of Mr. Savill's productions are in the British Museum, and writing of them the late J. Winter Jones, Esq., the librarian to the Museum, said, "They have a peculiar interest, and I am anxious to preserve them for the use of the National Library." Mr. Savill has also written articles for several Encyclopædias and Guide Books, notably the "Globe Encyclopædia," and the "Great Eastern Railway Panoramic Guide."

He is also a zealous member of the Ancient Order of Foresters and Secretary of the local Court, which has given substantial proof of its appreciation of his labours by a handsome testimonial.

Had it not been for the energetic exertions and persistent labours of Mr. J. W. Savill, against much opposition, the Custom of Dunmow would have been a thing of the past. He merits the esteem of all who delight in popular antiquities for maintaining one of the most historically interesting of the Customs of Merrie England. We hope he will live long and his days be passed pleasantly, and have leisure to attend to the Dunmow Custom, which he contends is a quaint and picturesque one, linking us with the misty ages of the past.

William Winters, Esq., F.R.H.S., who has contributed so much to the literature of Essex, has kindly favoured us with communications. It will also be observed we have extracted valuable information from Coller's "People's History of Essex," Wright's "History of Essex," and numerous other works. From the two well-conducted county papers, the *Chelmsford Chronicle,* and the *Essex Weekly News,* we obtained important matter. We have to thank Robert Chambers, Esq., of the firm of Messrs. W. & R. Chambers, for presenting us with illustrations, and William Tegg, Esq., F.R.H.S., for similar act of kindness.

We must not omit to state "The Dunmow Flitch of Bacon" formed the subject of one of our contributions to "The Old Stories Re-told," in the *Newcastle Weekly Chronicle,* and to the editor, W. E. Adams, Esq., we are under considerable obligations for allowing us to reproduce our paper, with additions, in book form.

To our numerous subscribers we tender our grateful thanks, and hope our efforts to please may not have failed.

WILLIAM ANDREWS.

10, *Colonial-street, Hull, July 3rd,* 1877.

HISTORY

OF THE

Dunmow Flitch of Bacon Custom.

————o————

In the days of yore was established at the Priory of Dunmow, Essex, the custom of presenting a flitch of Bacon to any married couple who could swear that neither of them in a twelvemonth and a day from their marriage had ever repented of his or her union. As to the time this custom originated we must go as far back as the middle ages, and to the period when men were making crusades and the English Commons had not a voice in the State. At that time religious houses abounded in this country. The one connected with our notice (that of the Priory of Dunmow) was founded in 1104 by the Lady Juga, sister of Ralph Baynard, who held the manor at the time of the Domesday Survey. The monastic buildings are now entirely razed to the ground. A little of the Priory Church remains, which formed the east end of the choir, and the present parish church of Little Dunmow. Here may be seen several monuments of great interest and in a good state of preservation ; among others is that of Lady Juga, the foundress, and also a sculptured figure in alabaster of the "fair Matilda," daughter of the second Walter Fitzwalter, renowned in legendary story as the wife of Robin Hood, and the object of the illicit passion of King John, who, it is stated, caused her to be poisoned for rejecting his addresses.

The learned antiquary, Sir William Dugdale (who was born in 1605 and died in 1686), in his "Monasticon," tells the story of the "fair Matilda," and, in allusion to the flitch of bacon, states:—"Robert Fitzwalter, who lived long beloved by King Henry, the son of King John (as also of all the realm), betook himself in his latter days to prayer and deeds of charity, and great and bountiful alms to the poor, kept great hospitality, and re-edified the decayed Priory of Dunmow, which Juga, a most devout and religious woman, had builded ; in which Priory arose a custom, began and instituted either by him or some of his ancestors, which is verified by the common saying or proverb, 'That he which repents him not of his marriage, either sleeping or waking, in a year and a day, may lawfully go to Dunmow and fetch a gammon of bacon.' It is certain that such a custom there was, and that the bacon was delivered with such solemnity and triumph as they of the Priory and town could make—continuing till the dissolution of that house. The party or pilgrim took the Oath before the Prior of the Convent, and the Oath was administered with long process and much solemn singing and chanting."

"The Vision of Piers Plowman," a religious allegorical satire, attributed to Robert Langlande, and written about 1362, contains a reference to the Dunmow flitch. In the following lines (which are slightly modernised to render them intelligible) the satirist adverts to the hasty and ill-assorted marriages that followed the great pestilence, the "black death" :—

> "Many a couple since the Pestilence
> Have plighted them together ;
> The fruit that they bring forth
> Is foul words,
> In jealousy without happiness,
> And quarrelling in bed ;
> They have no children but strife.
> And slapping between them :
> And though they go to Dunmow
> (Unless the Devil help !)
> To follow after the Flitch,
> They never obtain it ;
> And unless they both are perjured,
> They lose the Bacon."

In the "Prologue of the Wife of Bath's Tale," by Chaucer, the merry wife relates how she treated her husbands, and shows they had little chance of obtaining the prize of matrimonial felicity. She observes :—

> "The bacoun was nought fet for [t]hem, I trowe,
> That som men fecche in Essex at Dunmowe."

About the year 1445 appeared a theological poem, being a sort of paraphrase in verse of the Ten Commandments, and of which some extracts appear in "Reliquiæ Antiquæ." The author, commenting on the Seventh Commandment, bewails the corruption of the period that he could

> "——— find no man now that will inquire
> The perfect ways unto Dunmow,
> For they repent them within a year,
> And marry within a week, I trow."

Allusions to the custom have been found by Mr. Thomas Wright, M.A., F.S.A., in MSS. of the latter part of the sixteenth century at Oxford and Cambridge. Writing in 1650, Howell says:—

> " Do not fetch your wife from Dunmow
> For so you may bring home two sides of a sow."

Henry Bates, the son of a clergyman near Chelmsford, was the author of " The Flitch of Bacon," a ballad opera, acted at the Haymarket Theatre, 1778, and printed in 1779. We make a few selections from the piece:—

AIR XIII

" Ye good men and wives,
   Who have lov'd all your lives,
   And where vows have at no time been shaken,
   Now come and draw near,
   With your consciences' clear,
   And demand a large flitch of Bacon.
       Chorus—Ye good men and wives, &c.

" Since a year and a day
   Have in love roll'd away,
   And an oath of that love has been taken.
   On the sharp pointed stones,
   With your bare marrow bones,
   You have won our fam'd Priory Bacon.
       Chorus—Ye good men and wives, &c."

AIR IX.—DUET.

SHE—" Tho' fortune cloud hope's friendly ray
      That beams our guardian light,
      Our constancy shall cheer the day,
      Our love the longest night.
HE—By thee beloved !
SHE—   While blessed with thee
BOTH—Stern fate may frown in vain,
      Content and sweet simplicity
      Will take us in their train."

AIR XIV

" Ladies would you taste Love's Bacon
   But one way you'll ever find :
   Let the solemn vow you've taken
   With the body tie the mind.

" Mark but this, and we'll ensure ye
   To be ever blest and wise ;
   'Tis the charm that will secure ye
   Dunmow's matrimonial prize.

" And ye men, when you are joking,
   Scorn to trap our sex by art ;
   Nought to woman's so provoking
   As a hand without a heart."

AIR. XI.

"Odds bobs she's wondrous pretty !
Her locks are almost jetty !
She's a finer wench than Betty,
And see her eyes are blue.

"Her snow-white bosom's heaving !
My appetite is craving !
She hits my taste to a shaving !
Sweet damsel, how do you do ?"

Having lingered with the poets of the olden time, let us turn to prose. According to Morant, the historian of Essex, "the prior and canons were obliged to deliver the bacon to them that took the oath, by virtue (as many believe) of a founder or benefactors' deed or will, by which they held lands, rather than by their own singular frolic and wantonness, or more probably it was imposed by the Crown, either in Saxon or Norman times, and was a burthen upon the estate." It is stated that after the Pilgrims, as the claimants were termed, had taken the oath, they were taken through the town in a chair, on men's shoulders, with all the friars, brethren, and townsfolk, young and old, male and female, after them, with shouts and acclamations, and the bacon was borne before them on poles.

From the Chartulary of the Priory, which is deposited in the British Museum, it appears that only three couple obtained the bacon previous to the suppression of the religious houses. These were respectively on the 27th April, 1445, in the year 1468, and on the 8th of September, 1510. The following are taken from the original entries now in the British Museum :—

"MEMORANDUM.—That one Richard Wright, of Badbourge, near the city of Norwich, in the county of Norfolk, yeoman, came and required the bacon of Dunmow on the 27th day of April, in the 23rd year of the reign of King Henry VI., and according to the form of the charter, was sworn before John Cannon. Prior of this place and the convent, and many other neighbours, and there was delivered to him, the said Richard, one flitch of bacon."

"MEMORANDUM.—That one Stephen Samuel, of Little Easton, in the county of Essex, husbandman, came to the Priory of Dunmow, on our Lady day in Lent, in the seventh year of King Edward IV., and required a gammon of bacon, and was sworn before Roger Bulcott, then prior, and the convent of this place, as also before a multitude of other neighbours, and there was delivered to him a gammon of bacon."

"MEMORANDUM.—That in the year of our Lord, 1510, Thomas Le Fuller, of Coggeshall, in the county of Essex, came to the Priory of Dunmow, and on the 8th September, being Sunday, in the second year of King Henry VIII., he was, according to the form of the Charter, sworn before John Tils, the Prior of the house and convent, as also before a multitude of neighbours, and there was delivered to him, the said Thomas, a gammon of bacon."

In neither of the foregoing records, says D. W. Coller, in "The
People's History of Essex," will be observed any mention of the lady.
She does not seem to have been sworn. From all that appears to the
contrary, she was left at liberty to work her whims and indulge her temper; and the bacon was a reward for the patience of enduring husbands.
It appears from the language of one historian—and he has not been gain-
said—that the wife was not present. After describing the administration
of the oath, he says—"Then the pilgrim was taken on men's shoulders,
and carried first about the Priory Churchyard and after that through the
town with all the friars, brethren and townsfolk, with shouts and acclamations, with his bacon borne before him, and sent home in the same
manner." In modern times, however, the wife has been subjected to the
ordeal, to increase the difficulty of obtaining the prize, and thus to save
the bacon of the Lord of the Manor.

Although we have only particulars of three presentations prior to
the suppression of religious houses, we are disposed to believe more
claims were entertained and the register of them is lost. The frequent
allusions to the subject by our old poets support our supposition. Let us
hope the claimants were numerous and successful, and that many happy
lives were made happier by the rewards.

The Priory of Dunmow was, of course, amongst the religious
establishments suppressed by Henry the Eighth. Although the old
religion of the place was gone, the bacon was saved. We have to state
to the honour of the secular proprietors, they either held it as a solemn
engagement which they inherited with the land, or they appreciated the
old Custom and desired to maintain it. Particulars of the next presentation we gather from Morant, who obtained them from the rolls of the
court:—

At a Court Baron of Sir Thomas May, Knt., holden the 7th of June, 1701, before
Thomas Wheeler, gent., steward, the homage being five fair ladies, spinsters; namely,
Elizabeth Beaumont, Henrietta Beaumont, Annabella Beaumont, Jane Beaumont, and Mary
Wheeler.—They found that John Reynolds, of Hatfield Brodoke, gent. [Essex], and Ann
his wife; and William Parsley, of Much Easton [Essex], butcher, and Jane, his wife, by
means of their quiet and peaceable, tender and loving cohabitation for the space of three
years last past, and upwards, were fit and qualified persons to be admitted by the court
to receive the ancient and accustomed oath, whereby to entitle themselves to have the
Bacon of Dunmow delivered unto them according to Custom of the Manor. Accordingly,
having taken the oath, kneeling on the two great stones near the church door, the Bacon
was delivered to each couple.

Mr. John Reynolds was the Steward to Sir Charles Barrington.

The next claim was granted in the year of grace 1751, and the official account is as follows :—

The Manor of Dunmow late the Priory in Essex. { The Special Court Baron of Mary Hallett, Widow, Lady of the said Manor, there held for the said Manor, on Thursday, the twentieth day of June, in the five and twentieth year of the reign of our Soverign Lord George the Second, by the grace of God, of Great Britain, France, and Ireland, King, Defender of the Faith, and in the year of our Lord, One Thousand Seven Hundred and Fifty One, before George Comyns, Esquire, Steward of the said Manor.

HOMAGE.

William Towusend, Gent.
Mary Cater, Spinster.
John Strutt, the yor., Gent.
Martha Wickford, Spinster.
James Raymond, the yor., Gent.
Elizabeth Smith, Spinster.

Sworn.

Daniel Heckford, Gent.
Catherine Brett, Spinster.
Robert Mapletoft, Gent.
Eliza Haslefoot, Spinster.
Richard Birch, Gent.
Sarah Mapletoft, Spinster.

Be it remembered, that at this Court, it is found and presented by the homage aforesaid, that Thomas Shakeshaft, of Weathersfield, in the County of Essex, weaver, and Ann, his wife, have been married for the space of seven years last past and upwards. And it is likewise found, presented, and adjudged by the homage aforesaid, that the said Thomas Shakeshaft, and Ann. his wife, by means of their quiet, peaceable, tender, and loving cohabitation, for the space of time aforesaid, as appears to the said homage, are fit and qualified persons to be admitted by the Court to receive the ancient and accustomed Oath, whereby to entitle themselves to have the Bacon of Dunmow delivered unto them according to the custom of this manor. Whereupon at this Court, in full and open Court, came the said Thomas Shakeshaft and Ann, his wife, in their own proper persons, and humbly prayed they might be admitted to take the Oath aforesaid. Whereupon the said Steward, with the Jury, Suitors, and other Officers of the Court, proceeded with the usual solemnity to the ancient and accustomed place for the administration of the Oath, and receiving the bacon aforesaid (that is to say), to the two Great Stones lying near the Church door, within the said manor. where the said Thomas Shakeshaft, and Ann, his wife, kneeling down on the said two Stones, the said Steward did administer unto them the accustomed Oath, in the words or to the effect following, (that is to say) :—

You shall swear by custom of confession.
That you ne'er made nuptial transgression ;
Nor since you were married man and wife,
By household brawls or contentions strife.
Or otherwise at bed or at board.
Offended each other in deed or word ;
Or in a twelvemonth and a day,
Repented not in thought any way ;
Or since the parish clerk said "Amen,"
Wished yourselves unmarried again,
But continued true, and in desire,
As when you joined hands in holy quire,

And immediately thereupon the said Thomas Shakeshaft, and Ann, his wife, claiming the said bacon, the Court pronounced the sentence for the same in these words, or to the effect following to wit :—

Since to these conditions without any fear,
Of your own accord you do freely swear;
A whole gammon of bacon you shall receive,
And bear it away with love and good leave ;
For this is the custom of Dunmow well known,—
Tho' the pleasure be ours, the bacon's your own.

And accordingly a gammon of bacon was delivered to the said Thomas Shakeshaft, and Ann, his wife, with the usual solemnity.

An account of the presentation will be found in the *Gentleman's Magazine* and the old *London Magazine* for the year 1751, from which it appears that the successful candidates realised a large sum of money by selling slices of the bacon to those who witnessed the ceremony. It is estimated that some five thousand persons were present. David Ogborne, a local artist of the period, sketched the scene, and painted it. The picture is in the possession of Lieut.-Colonel William James Lucas, of Witham. The production is worthy of Hogarth. We are enabled to include an engraving of it from Chambers's "Book of Days." William Hone, in his "Every-Day Book," reproduces a print of great rarity, "sold by John Bowles, Map & Printseller, in Cornhill," entitled "The Manner of Claiming the Gammon of Bacon, &c., by Thos. Shakeshaft and Ann, his wife." William Tegg, Esq., F.R.H.S., a gentleman who has devoted considerable attention to the Dunmow custom, in his interesting volume, the "Knot Tied," kindly places at our disposal the illustration from Hone's book.

The antique chair in which the successful claimants were formerly carried is still preserved in the chancel of Little Dunmow church. Its dimensions are such as to bring the loving pair who may occupy it, in a rather close juxtaposition, It is undoubtedly of great antiquity, probably the official chair of the Prior, or that of the Lord of the Manor, in which he held his usual courts and received the suit and service of his tenants. It in no way differs from the chief chairs of ancient halls. We furnish an engraving of this interesting relic.

It is stated in a newspaper of the year 1772, that on the 12th June that year, John and Susan Gilder, of Terling, in Essex, made their public entry into Dunmow, escorted by a great concourse of people, and demanded the gammon of bacon, according to notice previously given, declaring themselves ready to take the usual oath; but to the great disappointment of the happy couple and their numerous attendants, the Priory gates were found fast nailed, and all admittance refused, in pursuance of the express orders of the Lord of the Manor.

For many years the ancient custom was numbered with things belonging to the past. Coming to more recent times, we find it stated by Mr. John Timbs, that "It is reported in the neighbourhood that when our excellent Queen had been married a year and a day, the then Lord of the Manor privately offered the Flitch of Bacon to her Majesty, who declined the compliment; but be it true or not, the same generosity was not extended to the less elevated claimants."

The next claim was made in the year 1851, particulars respecting it we gather from an account by Mr. Pavey; he tells us "Mr. and Mrs. Hurrell, owners and occupiers of a farm at Felsted, Essex, adjoining Little Dunmow, made claim to the Lord of the Manor of Dunmow Priory for the prize, but the application was not granted, the custom having been so long dormant.

When the refusal of the Lord of the Manor to comply with the ancient Custom became known to the inhabitants of Dunmow and the neighbourhood, an intimation was given to Mr. and Mrs. Hurrell that if they drove over to Easton Park, near Dunmow, on a day appointed for a Public Fête (the 16th July), they would receive there as a prize a Gammon of Bacon on taking the customary oath, and proving their title to the same. This notification being given to Mr. and Mrs. Hurrell, harmony was at once restored to the good folks of Dunmow, some of whom were afraid the Custom would be extinguished. A capital Brass Band was engaged, who mustered opposite the Town Hall, and when the happy couple arrived at the Market Cross, at Dunmow, they were received with joyful strains, as well as the acclamations of a large assemblage.

At three o'clock the neighbours and friends crowded to the Market Cross, at Dunmow, to accompany Mr. and Mrs. Hurrell to the Park, proving that the joyous couple possessed the hearty sympathy of all who knew them. The Procession set out; the musicians preceded the chaise containing the happy couple, playing "See the Conquering Hero Comes." Several banners and flags were borne along, and the Gammon of Bacon was carried in front, suspended from a pole adorned with ribbons.

The final destination of the Procession was the Rural Fête, in Easton Park, where the loving pair at length arrived, and were received with loud exclamations of welcome by the assembled crowd, including some of the aristocracy, gentry and yeomanry of the county, and were

TAKING THE OATH FOR THE GAMMON OF BACON,

By THOMAS SHAKESHAFT, *and* ANN, *his Wife, on June 20th,* 1751.

heartily congratulated with many a humourous compliment by all the married couples of whatever rank. About 3,000 persons were present. The Oath was duly administered to them by Mr. Pavey, and the loving pair received the Bacon amidst the tremendous cheering of the multitude, and they afterwards drove out of the Park Gates headed by the Band.

The evening closed with merry dances in the Park, and in the farm houses and cottages in the neighbourhood. The interesting ceremony on this occasion was productive of as much happiness and merriment as any of its predecessors, giving pleasure to both rich and poor, gentle and simple."

REVIVAL OF YE ANCIENT CUSTOM.

Shortly after the publication of the entertaining novel, entitled the "Flitch of Bacon," by W. Harrison Ainsworth, several of the inhabitants of Dunmow met, and, having formed a committee, agreed that the ancient Custom ought to be revived, and a resolution to that effect was passed. Particulars of the meeting having been communicated to Mr. Ainsworth, he replied as follows:—

I am happy to find I have been in some measure instrumental in reviving the good Custom of Dunmow. It will give me pleasure to co-operate with the Committee, and I beg to say I will gladly present a Flitch of Bacon to any couple who may claim it next summer, and who can justify their title to the prize. I shall also be happy to contribute five guineas towards the expenses of the entertainment on the occasion, which I feel certain will be well carried out.

After the receipt of the foregoing letter, the Committee again met, and it was agreed that the surplus of the receipts arising from the intended presentation of the Flitch should be given towards embellishing the Dunmow Town Hall, and furnishing that building with an illuminated clock. The following notice appeared in the local newspapers:—

Notice is hereby given, that all claimants for the Flitch of Bacon to be presented at Dunmow, in July, 1855, by Wm. Harrison Ainsworth, Esq., must forward their applications before the 24th June next, and attend per-

C

sonally at the Town Hall, Dunmow, to prove their title to the prize in open court. Such claimants and their witnesses will be examined before a jury of maidens and bachelors, and will be required to take the Oath according to old Custom. The successful candidates will be afterwards carried in procession to a fête to be held near the town. The Committee have to urge on claimants that the prize must not be estimated by its cost, but by the distinction it offers to those who may be fortunate enough to obtain it. Enviable are the wedded pair on whom the prize is conferred, since the acquisition establishes a claim of honour and respect. To say that a couple "deserve the Flitch" is a high compliment—to say that "they have actually won it," is to proclaim them amongst the best and happiest of mankind.—By order of the Committee,

CHARLES PAVEY.

After the appearance of the above announcement, numerous claims were made, and two couples were selected, namely, Mr. James Barlow and Hannah, his wife, of Chipping Ongar (where Mr. Barlow carried on business as a builder), and the Chevalier and Madame de Chatelain. M. de Chatelain is a French gentleman, who was married to an English lady, both of whom have gained distinction by their able contributions to our literature. We are enabled to furnish our readers with a copy of the letter addressed to Mr. Ainsworth by Madame Clara de Chatelain :—

Might I trouble you to inform me in what manner the candidates for the Flitch of Bacon, you propose offering to any couple on condition to take the necessary Oath, are to put themselves *sur les rangs* for obtaining this honour, presuming that in these days of mutual alliance no objection will arise on the score of one of the pair being a foreigner, especially as he is natural sed.

You must know that as far back as 1845, we applied for the Flitch at Little Dunmow, when the Lord of the Manor informed us the Custom had fallen into desuetude, and considered it would tend to no good to revive it ! Subsequently, we wrote three years ago to the rector, to inquire whether there was any truth in a newspaper account of a Flitch purporting to have been given at Little Dunmow, but he himself had only seen it in print, not in reality. At the same time, he very considerately hinted that I did not know all the disagreeables we should have to go through on such an occasion—instancing kneeling on sharp stones, &c., to say nothing of considerable fees, rather a formidable prospect for poor authors. Would you, therefore, be at the trouble, while informing me how to apply for the Flitch, to state whether all the old ceremonies are to be preserved, or are they to be modernised to suit the more fastidious taste of the 19th century ? At the same time, I must say we are not a couple to take alarm at trifles, and having steered clear of the shoals and quicksands of quarrel nearly twelve years of *ménage* (which people seem to think so difficult an achievement), it would not be a little that would prevent our becoming candidates for the coming glory of the Flitch.— With the Chevalier's best compliments, I remain, Sir, your obedient servant,

London, 3rd January, 1855. CLARA DE CHATELAIN.

July 19th, 1855, was the day appointed for reviving the ancient Custom. A chair of state, jury-boxes, seats for the claimants, witnesses, and counsel, had been prepared in the handsome little Town Hall, and profusely decorated with garlands of roses and other tasteful ornaments. The hall was well filled with spectators of both sexes, out of whom six maidens and six bachelors volunteered to act as jurors. At two o'clock Mr. William Harrison Ainsworth, as the donor of the Flitches, took the chair to preside over the court; the two sets of claimants, with their two witnesses each, were ushered into the places appropriated; and the counsel (consisting of Mr. Robert Bell, for the claimants, and Mr. Dudley Costello who opposed them) took their seats. The præco, or crier (Mr. Charles Pavey), with mock ceremony, opened the court, and Mr. Ainsworth, from the chair, delivered an appropriate address, in which he traced very lucidly all that is known of the history of this Custom; dwelt on the advantage of keeping up old Customs like this, which furnished innocent and exhilarating amusement to the people and tended to protect rather than endanger morality, and upon the injudicious but fruitless opposition which a party had made to it in the present instance. Amidst hearty cheers Mr. Ainsworth concluded his interesting address.

The jury having been charged, the fair members raising a laugh by pouring forth, in reply to the question whether they would well and truly try, &c., a rapid fusillade of "I wills"—probably thinking they were at the marriage altar—and the claimants being summoned to draw near, the ordeal of the day proceeded.

Mr. Robert Bell said he had now to open the case on the part of the claimants. They would have gathered from the address they had just heard, that it was the best and kindliest feelings this old Custom had been revived, and that it was carried out in sincerity and good faith. Like all such revivals, it was liable to derision and ridicule, and unfortunately the English were a sensitive people on that point; and this had no doubt deterred many from supporting Customs of this kind. But our ancestors were wiser in this respect than we were. They also were open to ridicule, but they were not so sensitive to its effects. Now in allusion to the establishment of this old Custom, he might observe that contemporaneously with it there existed in France, with men of gallantry and women of wit, an institution similar to this in the Courts of Love, of which they had all heard. They were tribunals for the adjudication of questions before marriage, similar to this after marriage; but he trusted it did not follow that love might not exist as purely and intensely in one state as in the other. (Cheers.) The Courts of Love were instituted in the twelfth century, and they exercised considerable influence on society; they existed and flourished in the time of the Troubadours for two hundred years, and when the Troubadours declined, the Courts of Love fell into disuse. These courts were presided over by the most distinguished persons, sometimes by eminent women, amongst whom would be found Queen Eléonore, the Viscountess Ermengarde of Narbonne, and the famous Countess of Champagne: sometimes by princes, and nobles, including in the illustrious roll the names of Richard Cœur de Lion, Alphonsus of Arragon, and the Dauphin of Auvergne. The main object of the institution was to regulate the intercourse of lovers, which, perhaps, it would be said, did not require regulation, as lovers were best left to themselves; but if any young lady had a slight or wrong to complain of, she here found prompt redress; if a gentleman had to complain of coldness or broken promises he preferred his complaint; the matter was investigated, and a verdict was pronounced that was held of as much authority as that of any judicial tribunal in the kingdom. To show the nature of these courts he would mention some of the cases brought before them. One was a case in which the lady bound her lover never to speak publicly in her praise; but on one occasion, hearing her assailed in company, he defended her, and pronounced an enthusiastic eulogium upon her. The lady brought him before the Court of Love, but it was held that the condition was illegal, and, therefore, not binding, the first and paramount duty of a gentleman in these circumstances being to defend the character of her to whom he was engaged; and the court condemned the lady to love him again more warmly than she did before. (Laughter.) Another was the case of a secretary who was employed to carry messages between two lovers; he fell in love with the lady, and supplanted the gentleman he represented. The decision of the court was that the secretary was worthy of the lady, and the lady of the secretary, and that neither of them were fit to be admitted into society again. (Laughter.) But to return to this Custom at Dunmow. Objections had been taken to it, as there were to all amusements, for there were some people who were always ready to

" Compound for sins they are inclined to,
By damning those they have no mind to."

(Laughter.) This ceremony was objected to because it would bring a large body of people together, and because there was likely to be a degree of hilarity amongst them which it was considered they ought not to enjoy ; but let them look back to the manner in which these things were treated in the time of the Commonwealth, and see the effect of it in the re-action that followed the Restoration. As to crowds coming together, he trusted to the good sense of the people not to make it the means of excess; and the people, he thought, might be safely left to themselves. (Cheers.) It had also been said that this was not a legitimate revival, because Little Dunmow, where the ceremony in olden times took place, was two miles from that spot. Now, there were Customs in which locality was an indispensable matter, but there were others in which it was not. For instance, if they undertook to visit a certain shrine they must make a pilgrimage to that particular spot. But this Custom was not a custom of locality—the place was an accident, not an essential. They had heard that it existed in Staffordshire, in Germany, and in France. Its essential element was its address to the human affections, and he was sure that they were not confined to a locality, and could be celebrated in Great as well as in Little Dunmow. (Cheers.) Where-ever there were true hearts and happy marriages, wherever people had love and trust, and could estimate the influence of woman on society— wherever these things were found, there they were in the right place, and above all they were particularly in the right place in Dunmow. (Cheers.) He now proceeded to the object of the day, and to draw attention to the claims of Mr. Barlow, and he thought it would be difficult to find in the class of society to which he belonged a case of a more interesting nature. He occupied a position to which he had risen by his own industry and perseverance. He began life in a humble situation, and had nothing to rely upon but his own unaided exertions; but his energy was great and he had conquered fortune. (Cheers.) He was now in circumstances creditable to himself and satisfactory for his friends to contemplate. A more admirable example of successful effort, and of a strict discharge of domestic and professional responsibilities could hardly be adduced than that which he should present to them when he called Mr. Barlow forward as the first witness in his own case. (Applause.)

Mr. Dudley Costello said his learned friend had performed to day what we knew must be to him an extremely pleasant duty—that of pre senting to this court no fewer than four claimants for participation in the time-honoured Custom of Dunmow. His duty, he regretted to say, was not of so agreeable a nature as that of his learned friend, but he should be happy, indeed, if in its performance he failed to invalidate the flatter ing statements his friend had made concerning the domestic happiness of his interesting clients. But while he gave utterance to this feeling, he was equally under the necessity of declaring that he could not suffer his assertions to go forth without examining their validity. The ladies and gentlemen of the jury might believe him that the purpose for which they were assembled here to-day was no trivial matter, no mere idle pastime of the hour, no slight or frivolous occasion, as some persons had not been backward to assert, but one that bore in the most direct and earnest way —though the manner of it might be homely—upon that which was the first object of our domestic care, the realisation of the joys and comforts of married life. To test the sincerity of those vows which declared at the altar that constant affection should ever prevail, and love, honour, and obedience be in turn faithfully rendered, the Custom at Dunmow— the history of which his lordship had so clearly and eloquently described —was originally instituted. That it had been a most successful institu tion the records of upwards of six hundred years sufficiently proclaimed.

He could not, as his lordship had observed, point out, at this distance of time, the earliest who did honour to the observance; neither could he indicate all the fortunate candidates, but that it was always a familiar institution they would know from the fact of its re-appearance at numerous intervals in the history of the county, and from this pertinent circumstance also, that the establishment of a claim to the Flitch was a proverbial expression for attaining the highest reach of domestic felicity. The purpose of the Custom was honest and true; and all those who in earnestness of heart had demanded and obtained the much coveted reward had themselves been living evidences of honesty and truth. They who came forward to claim the Flitch had a high object in view, the act itself being a public tribute to virtue; and the maintenance of the observance was virtue's recognition. It was, then, as the guardian of a Custom, whose tendencies were so ennobling, whose design was in every way so praiseworthy, that he made his appearance in this court. He entertained little doubt that his learned friend had, in both the instances which he intended to bring forward, what was termed a strong case, and his desire was to make each of them stronger by subjecting them to the ordeal of close inquiry. The field that was gained without a contest was one upon which no laurels grew worth wearing; that wreath alone was prized which it had cost them a struggle to obtain. (Cheers.)

Mr. James Barlow was then called, and, in answer to questions, said:—I live at Chipping Ongar, and have done so for twenty-three years; I was born in the parish of Shelly, and began life as a ploughboy there; I then went out for four years as factotum to a lady.

Mr. Bell: That was exceedingly good preparation for the position in which you are now placed. (Laughter.)

Mr. Barlow: I saved a little money and then apprenticed myself, and for nine years worked as journeyman, and then took the business of my brother-in-law, and I am tolerably satisfied with my position.

Mr. Bell: What was the mode you adopted—what was the secret of your success?

Mr. Barlow: I laid it down as a rule to do justice to everyone who employed me; I have suffered much from ill-health, but I have always found where there was a will there was a way, and when I could not give orders myself I wrote them; I have had losses from the villainy of a friend, but I did nothing to him; he is now in America, but from my own former good feeling I would not betray him.

Mr. Bell: Now turn to a delicate question. How long did you know Mrs. Barlow before you married her?—Four years; our courtship was carried on by letters, as we were a hundred miles apart, but seeing her good qualities, I selected her from several others.

You have heard that it was asserted by Sir Kenelm Digby that there is a sort of sympathetic powder that will make a person a hundred miles off love you. Did you use any of that love powder in your correspondence? (Laughter.) Have you ever had a quarrel with Mrs. Barlow?—Decidedly not.

You have differed in opinion, I suppose?—Not on any material point so as to create ill-feeling. When I have been sitting at tea, she has said "You have had three cups of tea," when I thought I had two. (Laughter.)

What did you say then?—I said very well, then, I would have no more. (Laughter.)

I suppose you perfectly well understood, from your knowledge of her character, what she meant when she said that you had had three cups of tea?—She had no wish to go into argument on the matter: the thing was settled. (Laughter.)

Did you ever differ from her on the subject of colours?—I think not.

You have had just differences as were sufficient to cause a little ruffle on the waters of life and keep them fresh?—Certainly not. Do you mean the first year of our marriage, or the whole fifteen years?

Ah, that is a legal point; I must leave it for the Judge to decide. (Laughter.) When did you think of claiming the Flitch?—I always had my eye on the matter.

Now, have you ever felt a passing pang of jealously, though not expressed it?—Certainly not.

What were the feelings of your friends when you claimed the bacon?
—Some approved and some joked us about it; there has been a degree
of ill-feeling, and I suppose it was envy. (Laughter.) I think, generally
speaking, this movement is popular amongst what I call the aristocracy
of the county, and the only persons who turn it into jeers are people of
my own class.

You never regretted your marriage?—Certainly not; my only objection is that the years flow by too quickly. (Laughter.)

Cross-examined by Mr. Costello: I came early to Dunmow this
morning, and I got up early to get ready for that purpose.

And when you were prepared was Mrs. B quite ready?—I believe
she was ready first. (Laughter.)

Now, are you sure that the Flitch itself was not the chief object
that brought you here to-day? Man's appetite is frail; are you not in
reality fond of bacon?—I don't much care about it.

Is not Mrs. B?—I dare say she would like a rasher.

Does she prefer it fried? You know there have been quarrels on
this point, which are recorded in a well-known song.—I never inquired in
what way she preferred her bacon. (Laughter.)

Are you in the habit of carrying an umbrella?—I am.

Was that umbrella, when you were going out in a hurry, ever mis-
laid?—It may have been.

And what did you do then?—I hunted for it. (Laughter.)

Without losing your temper?—Just so. (Laughter.)

Is Mrs. B in the habit of doing up her back hair of a night?
(Laughter.)

Mr. Bell objected to this question. Back hair was a mystery of the
toilet, and entitled to protection, like a privileged communication.

In the cold winter nights which we had a few months ago, did you,
before Mrs. B was ready to retire—did you, I ask, enter the nuptial
couch and warm Mrs. B's place for her?—Sometimes she was in bed
first. (Laughter.)

The President thought this examination could not be pursued
further.

D

Mrs. Barlow was then called and asked, Did Mr. B fall in love with her, or she with him?—He with me, of course. (Laughter.)

Now, it is said that a lady has always one secret that she calls her own; had you that secret that you did not tell Mr. Barlow?—I never had any secret from my husband; he is of a lively temper to me. I recollect him in periods of suffering, depression, and illness, and I never saw any variation in his temper; I never regretted my marriage with him.

Cross-examined: It annoys me to see the house dirtied after it has been done up with care; but on such a day as this, if Mr. B comes in and leaves the marks of his dirty feet on the carpet I don't mind it. (Laughter.) He has kept dinner waiting, but I have never said "Goodness gracious, James, I wish you would consider other people," because I knew he was about his business and my interests.

Now, do your chimneys ever smoke?—Sometimes.

Your husband is a builder, and have you ever observed to Mr. Barlow that you thought he might have done something to prevent that?—Never.

Then you have no great faith in Mr. Barlow's abilities in that way? (Laughter.) Now, as to the keys.

Mr. Bell objected to the question. The keys were always held sacred in the ladies' possession, and his friend had no right to make use of them to unlock the secrets of married life. (Laughter.)

Mary Ann Clarke had known Mr. and Mrs. Barlow a long time, and never heard them say an angry word to each another.

Do you believe that they have conspired for fifteen years to make one another as happy as they could, merely to claim this bacon?—I did not know that they had any idea of claiming it.

Cross-examined: I have seen Mrs. B in a new bonnet, but I never heard it suggested that the purchase of that bonnet was the result of a compromise of a quarrel.

You know that famous song in which the quarrel between a couple, namesake of yours, led to the loss of the Flitch?—Oh yes, sir! my husband has often sung it to me, delightful!

And no such dispute ever arose between Mr. and Mrs. Barlow?—
Never to my knowledge.

Have you ever dined with the Barlows?—I can't say I have dined,
but I have often tea'd and supper'd with them.

William Nicholas, governor of the Ongar Union-house, thought Mr.
and Mrs. Barlow were a very happy couple, and justly entitled to the
Flitch.

Cross-examined: I have had a hand at whist with them, and they
have been partners and Mrs. B may have trumped Mr. B's ace, and he
has kept his temper. (Laughter.)

Did you ever see a suspicious-looking stick hanging up behind Mr.
B's door?

Witness: A ground ash?

Mr. Costello: No, I should say a crab rather.—Never.

Mr. Costello then said there was nothing struck him in the matter
to induce him to resist the claim, except those suspicious three cups of
tea. If his friend could reconcile that he should be content.

Mr. Bell submitted that the very circumstances relating to the three
cups of tea was in itself a proof of Mr. Barlow's docility of temper;
and he appealed to that low sweet voice they heard in Mrs. B, which he
was sure must have made such an impression on the Jury as to ensure a
verdict in their favour.

Mr. Ainsworth said he thought the case was sufficiently made out,
but it was for the Jury to decide.

The Jury found unanimously that the Claimants were entitled, and
the announcement was received with rounds of cheers.

THE CHEVALIER AND MADAME DE CHATELAIN'S CLAIM.

Mr. Bell then opened the case for M. de Chatelain, who, he said, was
a gentleman distinguished by his literary attainments—whose pursuits
were literary, as were also those of his lady; and he looked on it as a
healthy sign of public opinion that a man like him should come forward
to claim the Flitch, for it gave interest as well as sanction to this time-
honoured custom.

M. de Chatelain was then examined, and he stated that he came from Paris and met Madame in London, and had been married to her for twelve years; his pursuits were literary and so were those of Madame, and he found the idea a fallacy that a clever woman did not make a good wife.

Mr. Bell : Was this a love match ?

M. de Chatelain : Oh, certainly. (Laughter.) In fact I fell in love with personal beauty and mental endowments, and I have no reason to lament my marriage, or to suppose that my first estimate of Madame was to high; on the contrary, I find her a much more excellent person than I supposed her to be. We never had any difference; we have lived in France, but the difference in habits did not lead to any difference of opinion.

Cross-examined : Never had any difference of opinion on political subjects. He admired all Englishwomen, but loved one.

Madame de Chatelain : I have heard M. de Chatelain's evidence, and I concur in what he has stated ; I have never found occasion, in any instance, to regret my marriage ; we always write in one room, and we are able to compose much better than if we write alone ; I do not entertain the notion that women ought to be returned to Parliament; I do not think it necessary that ladies should be called in to assist in making laws ; I think woman's proper duty lies at home, and in performing her domestic duties she best fulfils her mission.

Cross-examined : I was married in England, and promised to obey— the French service, I think, has the same promise, but I am not sure; and I have never found it grating or unpleasant to do anything that I have been told by M. de Chatelain.

Miss Kearskey, a portrait painter, said in her profession she had studied physiognomy, and she had formed an opinion of gentleness and good temper from Madame's face ; had known them sixteen years, but had never known them quarrel, and thought they were, in fact, a profoundly happy pair.

M. Donné said he came from Normandy, and had known M. de Chatelain thirty years ; he looked better and happier since his marriage, which he attributed to his happiness in that state. (Laughter.) Had never seen an instance of unpleasantness between them ; they were always cheerful, ever good tempered, and ever united.

Cross-examined: Had dined *en garcon* with M. de Chatelain, but never heard him singing "We won't go home till morning." (Laughter.)

Mr. Costello was so satisfied with the evidence that he had nothing to say against the claim.

Mr. Bell called attention to the fact that the proofs were so strong that his friend despaired of shaking them, and it was therefore unnecessary for him to address the Jury.

The maidens and bachelors found for the claimants, and amidst plaudits and congratulations the proceedings in the Town Hall closed.

The president, jurors, &c., left the Court, and, amidst the multitude without, a procession was formed in the following order :—

Marshal.

Stud of horses, mounted by yeoman in appropriate dresses, carrying banners, with the names of all the claimants since the 13th century inscribed on them and the arms of persons associated with the custom.

Ladies with garlands.

Banners borne by rustics borne uniformly.

Maidens and bachelors of the jury in a carriage.

The Clerk of the Court, the Crier of Court, the Counsel in a Carriage.

Other officers of the Court.

Gentlemen with wands, walking.

Flitch of Bacon borne by four yeoman.

Band.

Officers of the Court and gentlemen with wands.

Mr. and Mrs. Barlow, carried on a chair on men's shoulders.

Gentlemen with wands.

Banners borne by rustics.

Two minstrels playing pipe and tabor.

Flitch of Bacon.

Band.

Le Chevalier and Madame de Chatelain, carried on a chair on men's shoulders.

Mr. William Harrison Ainsworth in a carriage.

The procession took its course through the principal streets of the town, halting at the market cross, where the proclamation was made by sound of trumpet and drum that the flitches had been adjudged to the respective claimants, and would be publicly delivered to them in the field. The party then proceeded to a neighbouring field, where a large pavilion had been erected. A stage was placed inside the tent for the officers, counsel, and claimants. After a solemn declaration had been made by each claimant, who knelt down on stones prepared for them, Mr. Ainsworth delivered to each couple a flitch of bacon. In mock, official form the following record was made :—

Town Hall, Dunmow.

The Special Court here, held on Thursday, the 19th day of July, in the 19th year of the reign of our Sovereign Lady Victoria, by Grace of God of Great Britain and Ireland, Queen, Defender of the Faith, and in the year of our Lord one thousand eight hundred and fifty-five, before William Harrison Ainsworth, Esquire.

Jury.

Maidens.   Bachelors.

Be it remembered that at this Court it is found and presented that Jean Baptiste Francois Ernest de Chatelain, of Grafton Place, Euston Square, London, author, and Clara, his wife, have been married for the space of twelve years last past and upwards. And it is likewise found, presented and adjudged by the Court that the said Jean Bap. Fr. Ernest de Chatelain, and Clara, his wife, by means of their quiet, peaceable, tonder, and loving cohabitation for the space of time aforesaid, are fit and qualified persons to be admitted by the Court to have the Bacon of Dunmow delivered to them according to custom. Whereupon at this Court, in full and open Court, came the said J. B. F. Ernest de Chatelian and Clara, his wife, in their own proper persons, and humbly prayed they might be admitted to make their solemn declaration ; and the said W. H. Ainsworth, with the jury, witnesses, and officers of the court, having heard the evidence adduced and counsel on both sides, adjudged the said J. B. F. Ernest de Chatelain and Clara, his wife entitled to claim the said Flitch of Bacon, and with the claimants proceeded with the usual solemnity to the place for administration of the declaration, and receiving the bacon aforesaid, that is to say, to two great stones in Windmill Field, Dunmow, aforesaid, where the said J. B. F. Ernest de Chatelain and Clara, his wife, kneeling down on these said two stones, Charles Pavy, clerk of the court, did administer unto them the accustomed solemn declaration [in nearly the same words as before given].

And immediately thereupon the said J. B. F. Ernest de Chatelain, and Clara his wife, claiming the said bacon, the court pronounced the sentence for the same in these words, or to the effect following (to wit) :—

> Since to these conditions without any fear,
> Of your own accord you do freely declare,
> A whole flitch of bacon you shall receive,
> And bear it hence with love and good leave ;
> For this is our custom, at Dunmow well known,— ·
> Though the pleasure be ours the bacon's your own.

—In pursuance of which a flitch of bacon was publicly delivered by the said W. H. Harrison, Esq., to the said J. B. F. Ernest de Chatelain, and Clara, his wife, in Windmill Field, Dunmow aforesaid, with usual solemnity, on the day and year before mentioned.

(Signed)

JEAN BAPTISTE F. ERNEST DE CHATELAIN, } Claimants.
CLARA DE CHATELAIN,

W. HARRISON AINSWORTH, Donor.

CHARLES PAVEY, Clerk of the Court.

A similar record was made as to the two other claimants, Mr. and Mrs. Barlow.

The remainder of the day until a late hour, was passed in various sports and amusements, for which ample provision had been made.

PRESENTATION IN 1857.

On the 25th of June, 1857, the town of Dunmow presented a lively appearance ; banners were flying and triumphal arches were erected. The day was selected for hearing the claims for the Flitch of Jeremiah

Heard, and Sarah, his wife, of Bentley, Staffordshire, also that of John
Nichol Hawkins, M.D., and Ann Sophia, his wife, of Victoria-place,
Regent's Park, London. The proceedings commenced in the Town Hall,
which had been tastefully decorated for the occasion. Mr. Barlow, a
former recipient of the Bacon, having, as Crier of the Court, proclaimed
silence,

Mr. William Harrison Ainsworth said: Two years ago we met
together in this place for the purpose of reviving the good old Custom of
Dunmow. And a very old Custom it is, as was then shown. Instituted
in the twelfth century, it has endured for upwards of 700 years. It
would be a thousand pities if an observance of such great antiquity, of
a character so quaint and picturesque, and fraught with so many genial
and poetical associations, should be allowed to become obsolete. Happily
there is now no danger of such a result. The Lord of the Manor of
Little Dunmow may neglect to keep up his charter, and refuse to furnish
a Flitch of Bacon to such as shall justly demand it. The appeal will be
answered here, and in this way. An estimable and kind-hearted lady,
whose name, when it is revealed to them, must always be held in grateful respect by the inhabitants of Dunmow, has intimated to the
authorities of the town her intention of bequeathing a sum of money
sufficient for the annual celebration of the Custom of the Flitch. A
noble action, and all honour to her for it. Her generosity will not be
misapplied. Thousands will be made happier for the holiday *fete* this
provision will afford them. And many a fondly-attached couple—held
up by her means as examples of conjugal felicity—will have reason to
bless the memory of this beneficent lady. Again I say all honour to her.
Thus the ancient custom of Dunmow, which it has been my good
fortune to assist in reviving, may be considered as perpetuated. Whatever may have been the origin of the old Custom, whether its design
was serious or jocular, or, as is more likely, a mixture of both, there can
be no doubt that, viewed in a proper light, its tendencies are beneficial.
A prize is offered for strict matrimonial good conduct—such good conduct
to be solemnly asserted by the claimants, and confirmed by witnesses.
Hence, examples are afforded best worthy of imitation of all married

THE DUNMOW PROCESSION,

June 20th, 1751, from a painting of the time, by DAVID OGBORNE.

folk. At a season like the present, when grave and perplexing questions of divorce are agitating our legislators, we may indeed congratulate ourselves that in this quiet little town of Essex we are far more agreeably occupied in seeking to lighten the matrimonial links instead of to undo them, our grand aim being to encourage wedded love and fidelity, and obviate the necessity of divorce. Loving couples will always find welcome and honour at Dunmow. And now in the language of an advertisement, which must have caught the eye of most of my readers, let me address myself "To those about to marry," and I hope there are many such here. I do not mean to recommend to them incredibly cheap furniture, nor any other indispensable household article, but to offer them a word of advice. *Avoid your first quarrel.* In the careful observances of this precept lies the secret of conjugal happiness. Act up to it, and you will be entitled to the Dunmow Flitch.

[Mr. Ainsworth sat down amidst the applause of the assembly.]

The Crier next advanced to the jury-box, and six maidens and six bachelors were empanelled.

Mr. Bowker then, in due form, proceeded to open the case, announcing that he had the honour of appearing as the advocate of both the parties coveting the Flitch, and expressing his regret that this cause had not fallen into the hands of one more deeply read in matrimonial history; but he had no doubt the parties believed their claims to be so clear that they felt they would be adequately advocated even by his humble ability. The claimants now before the Court were Thomas Jeremiah Heard and Sarah, his wife, and John Nichol Hawkins and Ann Sophia, his wife. As to the ancient custom of the Flitch he found that nine times had there been claims put in for it, and of these nine parties seven were natives of Essex, so at all events Essex was rather celebrated for matrimonial felicity. With regard to the first claimant, Mr. Heard, he was instructed to say he was now in the Staffordshire constabulary. He was born at Seckford-hall, but was now a peace officer, and he had shown that he not only kept the peace towards all Her Majesty's subjects but towards his wife, and that was the reason of his claim. As to Mr. and Mrs. Hawkins, they did not reside here but in Regent's Park; their

E

marriage was celebrated in Jersey, and as to their conjugal felicity he should produce evidence which he believed would be found satisfactory.

Mr. Costello subjected the claimants and their witnesses to a rigorous cross-examination.

The President thought both claims had been made out, but left the jury to decide which should be preferred.

The maidens and bachelors decided in favour of the happy pair from Staffordshire. The proceedings in the Town-hall closed. A procession was next formed in the following order:—

Marshal on Horseback.
Two Bands of Music.
Banners with names of the successful Claimants from the year 1445 to the present time, Coats of Arms of the Founder of the Custom, and those who assisted in its revival, Arms of the principal Landowners in Dunmow and the vicinity.
THE FLITCH OF BACON SUSPENDED ON FOUR POLES
(Securely guarded against any attacks of the hungry).
Garlands and devices in Flowers.
MR. AND MRS. HEARD IN A CHAIR BORNE BY EIGHT MEN
(Bowing and Smiling to the Salutations from Pavement and Window).
Jury of Maidens and Bachelors, in open Carriage, drawn by Four Horses.
Carriage containing Mr. and Mrs. Hawkins (trying to be satisfied as if they had secured the flitch) and witnesses.
Carriage containing the Officers of the Court.*

The procession, after passing through the town, halted at a meadow at the eastern extremity thereof. A large company, including the families of some of the neighbouring gentry, were assembled to witness Mr. Barlow administer the ancient oath. The rite fulfilled, the bacon was duly presented by Mr. Ainsworth, and a silver testimonial to Mr. and Mrs. Hawkins as a consolation prize.

Cheers were given to the claimants. Mr. Barlow proposed the best thanks of those present to Mr. Ainsworth. This was carried with three rounds of cheers. Mr. Ainsworth briefly acknowledged the compliment expressing a hope they would often be present on future occasions.

It is stated in the *Chelmsford Chronicle* as follows. "We have been requested to insert the following: Mr. Sparke, of Saffron Walden, desires it to be distinctly understood by the public that he and his wife were attending at Dunmow, ready to come forward in case no other claimants had appeared; and, it was illness alone that made his wife wish to defer the honour, but ill as she felt herself, she was ready (if needed) to go through all the formalities, and the secretary to the committee had an intimation to that effect previously to the proceedings of the day commencing."

Archery and various rustic sports kept alive the holiday till dusk. In respect to the bequest named by Mr. Ainsworth, in his opening address, we have to state as yet the committee has not heard anything more respecting it, although a leading firm of London solicitors corresponded some time with Mr. C. Pavey on the subject. Mr. J. W. Savill kindly submitted the letters to us, but we think they are not of sufficient general interest for publication.

PRESENTATION IN 1869.

This year Mr. J. W. Savill, although greatly opposed by several of the inhabitants of Dunmow carried out the festival most successfully. It would appear these people could not enter into the enjoyment of the revival of the old ceremony, nor feel satisfied at seeing others do so. We can only presume their own domestic bliss is not complete, and that they therefore think others are equally unfortunate. In answer to the advertisements for claimants a number of applications were received. The committee selected two, William Casson and Emma Elizabeth, his wife, of No. 3, Cornwall-road, Victoria Park, London, wood engraver; and Josiah Leaver and Mary Jane, his wife, of Rydon Cresent, Clerkenwell, London, jeweller. The day fixed for the presentation was the 16th of

August, 1869. H. Brinsley Sheridan, Esq., M.P. for Dudley (a member of the famous literary family), was announced to preside, but could not keep his appointments on account of the indisposition of his daughter. He wrote as follows:—

> · "17, Westbourne Terrace, Hyde Park, W.
>
> 10th August, 1869.
>
> I regret exceedingly that I shall be unable to take any part in the Dunmow ceremony, having to leave England for Germany (where I have a sick daughter) at the end of the week. It would otherwise have given me great pleasure to accept the invitation to witness the old English custom of giving the flitch.
>
> H. B. SHERIDAN."

Mr. E. T. Smith, a gentleman well known in the theatrical world, occupied the chair. Mr. Garden, of the Lyceum Theatre, London, represented the claimants, while Mr. Brooks opposed them. Mr. J. W. Savill acted as crier of the court. It was stated both sets of claimants had enjoyed four years of married life, and that Mrs. Casson had presented her husband with four children. Mrs. Leaver had not any family. After an amusing investigation, the jury of maidens and bachelors declared both parties entitled to the prizes. After the ancient oath had been taken the flitches were presented to the claimants. Over 20,000 persons witnessed the interesting ceremony. Mr. Smith provided various entertainments, which were, according to the Essex journals much appreciated by the visitors.

PRESENTATION IN 1874.

On Monday, August 10, 1874, was held the next presentation of the Dunmow Flitch. From numerous claimants, the committee selected Joseph James Clegg, and Hannah his wife, of 240, Roman-road, London. They were married at Prestwich parish church, Lancashire, on the 12th Feburary, 1861, and had been favoured with five children, four of whom were living. Mr. Clegg was employed as a clerk. The papers described Mr. and Mrs. Clegg as a most amiable looking couple.

Mr. William Casson a successful claimant of 1869, presided. Mr.

J. W. Savill took an active part in the trial. After numerous questions and satisfactory replies the mixed jury declared the claimants were entitled to the prize. After the ancient oath had been administered by Mr. Savill the happy pair received the Dunmow flitch. To add to the pleasure of the visitors various amusements were provided. The proceedings, which were conducted in a most satisfactory manner reflected great credit on the secretary, Mr. J. W. Savill.

The members of the local lodge of Foresters, known as the "Court of Prince Arthur," took part in the celebration, and the profits obtained by means of the entertainments were handed over to their funds.

PRESENTATION IN 1876.

Under the able management of Mr. J. W. Savill, on the 17th July, 1876, the Dunmow Flitch was again presented. Two claims were sent in, the claimants being the Rev. S. M. Smith, Vicar of Harwell, Berks, and his wife; and Mr. and Mrs. Boosey, parish clerk of Holy Trinity Church, Ventnor, Isle of Wight. We regret to state that Mr. Smith's engagements prevented him attending at Dunmow. He wrote Mr. Savill, under date of June 23, 1876, as follows:—

"Thank you very much for your letter of the 20th, but before its arrival I had made an engagement for the 17th of July and following days which I cannot recall. I am sorry it should be so, but if you will kindly write early to me some future occasion I will immediately put myself in communication with you, and endeavour to obtain the Flitch."

At the invitation of the Committee the writer of this little book had the pleasure of presiding. We did our best, in our opening address, to trace the history of the ancient Custom, and concluded by saying:—

"You must, I think, all feel with me that the meeting to-day is well calculated to promote matrimonial happiness. We are the great rival of the Divorce Court. The name of Dunmow and the remembrance of the Flitch causes the votaries of that court to hide in shame their heads. By the Committee I am directed to state that they urge on claimants to remember that the prize must not be estimated by its cost, but by the distinction it offers to those who may be fortunate enough to obtain it. Enviable are the wedded pair on whom the prize is conferred, since the acquisition establishes a claim of honour and respect. To say that a couple " deserve the Flitch" is a high compliment, to say that "they have actually won it" is to proclaim them among the best and happiest of mankind."

Mr. Boosey and his spouse answered, in a most satisfactory manner, numerous questions submitted by the President and Mr. J. W. Savill, who appeared to save the Bacon of Dunmow, and failed in the attempt, certainly not for want of eloquence, nor did his remarks fall flat for want of humour. It was stated the happy pair had been married three years. James Henry Boosey was born at Standon, Herts, and Mary, his wife, at Furneux Pelham, in the same county. He was thirty-four years of age, and his good lady two years elder. A number of excellent testimonials as to their domestic felicity were submitted, amongst them one from the Vicar of the parish where the couple were married and now reside. When the question was put to the jury of maidens and bachelors whether they deemed the claimants entitled to the prize, they answered in the affirmative. After being chaired to the two sharp stones, kneeling thereon, and the oath had been taken, the Flitch was duly presented to them. We are disposed to think a more worthy pair never obtained the reward.

To add to the pleasure of the day Mr. Savill provided suitable and attractive amusements.

BIOGRAPHICAL AND HISTORICAL NOTES.

In tracing the History of the Dunmow Custom we have mentioned several notable persons. We think it will not be without interest to furnish a few biographical notes respecting some of them, also other matters bearing on the ceremony.

THE BAYNARD FAMILY.

Previous to the Conquest Little Dunmow was held by a freewoman, a freeman, and a sochman, and at the time of the Domesday Survey i belonged to Ralph Baignard or Baynard, who was also Lord of the Manor of Ashdon Hall, and forty other manors in Essex. The family had settled at Messing in the time of Henry III., and was possessed of the Manor there called after the family name. Lady Juga was a descendant of this family, and sister to Ralph, but nothing is known of her Ladyship beyond the fact of her founding the Priory of Little Dunmow in 1104. Geofrey Baynard succeeded his father Ralph. Geofrey's son, William, succeeded him, and inherited the large paternal estates in the county, but was deprived of the barony and whole estates for alleged treason against King Henry I., and in 1111 they were given by the King (Henry I.) to Robert, a young son of Richard Fitz-Gislebert, and from whom the noble family of Fitz-Walter descended.

THE FITZ-WALTERS.

On the forfeiture of William, the grandson of Ralph Baynard, the Barony and lordships passed by gift to Robert Fitz-Gislebert, the son of Richard (progenitor of the ancient Earls of Clare), from whom they descended to the Fitz-Walters, whose posterity held the lordship of Little Dunmow, and Woodham-Walter, as part of the Barony of Fitz-Walter, through ten generations down to 1464, when, in defect of heirs male, it was divided among co-heiresses. Robert, surnamed Fitz-Richard, died in 1134, leaving, by his wife, Maud, daughter of Simon de St. Liz, Earl of Huntingdon, his son and heir, Walter Fitz-Robert, who married Maud, eldest daughter of Richard de Lucy, by whom he had Robert Fitz-Walter, the second of the name, and distinguished in English history by his zealously appearing against King John, as General of the army of the English Barons, under the title of "Marechal of the Army of God and Holy Church," when the famous Magna Charta was wrung from King John in 1215, on the plains of Runnymede. This Robert Fiz-Walter is credited with instituting the famous "Custom of Dunmow." Mr. J. W. Savill, of Dunmow, to whom we are indebted for the successful revivals of the custom, is very strongly confirmed in his belief that Robert Fitz-Walter was the actual founder of the Dunmow Flitch, and claims for it a national interest on the great historical association connected with the founder as above narrated. Robert died in 1234, and was buried before the high altar in the Priory Church of Little Dunmow, which was the ancient burial place of the Fitz-Walter family. The Fitz-Walters have played a prominent part in Essex in bygone years. John was summoned to Parliament from 1341 to 1360. He married Alianor, daughter of Henry, Lord Percy, by whom he had Walter, born in 1345. He was actively engaged against the rebels in Essex, under Jack Straw, and served in Parliament from 1369 to 1385, and died in 1386. Walter, his son, also sat in Parliament from 1390 to 1403, and Walter the son of Walter also sat in the House two years. John the son of Thomas Ratcliffe, Esq., who had married Annie Fitzwalter, was summoned to Parliament by the title of Lord Fitzwalter in 1485. He was convicted of high treason in 1494, in joining the conspiracy to place Perkin Warbeck on the throne. He was carried to Calais and there beheaded. He was steward of the household of Henry VII. But his son Robert was restored to the honour of Lord Fitzwalter in 1505. He was created Viscount in 1525, and Earl of Sussex in 1529. * He married Elizabeth, a daughter of the Duke of Buckingham, by whom he had issue. Henry, his eldest son and successor, was K.B. and K.G.L., and married first Elizabeth, daughter of Thomas Howard, Duke of Norfolk. Frances, a daughter, married Sir Thomas Mildmay, of Moulsham, Chelmsford, who also held the Manor of Little Dunmow; and the above family still exists in Essex. On Henry's decease, in 1556, he was succeeded by his son. Thomas, Earl of Sussex and Lord-Deputy of Ireland, having obtained a grant of New Hall, † Boreham, a royal residence of Henry VIII., he made it his place of residence. He died without issue in 1583, and was interred in the chapel of Boreham Church. His widow

* By letters patent of King Henry VIII. we find he " granted to Robert, Earl of Sussex, and his heirs, the site of the priory of Dunmow, with the manors of Dunmow Parva and Clopton." "Clopton," or Clapton Hall was formerly held by the progenitors of Messrs. Fitch and Son (purveyors to H.R.H. the Prince of Wales), of Bishops-gate, London, who have generously responded to Mr. Savill's applications, and placed the " Flitches" at his disposal for the recent presentations, according to the " Custom of Dunmow." This curious coincidence is worthy of notice, and very creditable to the generosity of the descendants of their Dunmowian sires.

† New Hall has for many years been the habitation of the Conventual Order of the Nuns of the Holy Sepulchre, and is of great historic interest.—*Vide Coller's History Essex.*

The Chair in which the Couples obtaining the
Bacon were formerly carried.

was foundress of Sidney-Sussex College, Cambridge. His next brother, Henry, succeeded him; and he, in turn, was succeeded by his only child, Robert, Earl of Sussex, who died without issue. The last Lord Fitz-walter died about two years ago.

THE LITTLE DUNMOW PRIORY.

The Evangelical counsels of voluntary poverty, perpetual chastity, and entire obedience, have, in all ages of the Catholic Church, found many practical adherents. So great was the desire to embrace the Monastic and Conventual life at one period, that, had it being indiscriminately encouraged, it would have had a serious effect upon the population of the world, hence St. Francis founded his third order, which enabled Christians living in the world the advantages of the religious orders. Essex contained no less than 47 religious houses, of which the Priory of Dunmow was one. It was founded in the year 1104 for canons of the Augustine Order, by the Lady Juga, the sister of Ralph Baynard; and there was a manor belonging to it. Of Lady Juga nothing more is known beyond the fact that her name has been preserved by history as the foundress of the priory. The probability is that she entered upon a religious life herself, and died in peaceful seclusion. Of the extensive buildings belonging to this celebrated monastic institution, but a small portion has been preserved. The priory church was a large and stately fabric. It was consecrated by Maurice, Bishop of London, and dedicated to the B. Virgin (St. Mary.) The small portion preserved has been made to constitute the little parish church of the present plebeian villagers, and is merely the east end of the former choir, which formed either a south aisle of the chancel or of the nave of the ancient church now passed away. There is five arches in the north wall, of which the pillars have been preserved. Its massive columns and capitals, covered with rich carvings of oak foliage on the one side, and its beautiful traceried Gothic windows on the other, all attest the magnificence of this stately fabric, when entire in its pristine glory. A tomb under an arch in the south wall is believed to contain the remains of Lady Juga, the foundress. It is of chest like form, and of great apparent antiquity. The monuments have been preserved on the north side of the church; one to the memory
F

of Walter Fitzwalter (the first of the name), who died 1168, and was
buried with one of his wives in the middle of the choir. The figure of
Sir Walter has received considerable damage, and both legs are broken
off at the knees. The hair of the head has a singular appearance, radiat-
ing from a centre and curling inwards—a fashion observable in monuments of the same period. Sir Walter is represented in plate armour,
under which a shirt of mail is seen above the collar and below the skirts.
The mitre-like head dress of his lady, with lace, a necklace, and ear-rings,
gives a correct idea of the fashionable ornaments of high life of that age,
and come in for a good share of criticism by the feminine portion of
visitors, who flaunt their dainty tresses and toss a somewhat prettier
head-gear, and congratulate themselves that they escaped life in that age
when fashion would have forced them to have made such "horrid guys"
of themselves! "Ferdy, the idea!" Ferdy catches the echo, and exclaims " What, Dear?" Others of the noble house of Fitzwalter were
also buried here, particularly Robert, the founder of the ancient custom,
who, as has been said, was buried before the high altar, a special place of
honour, to the name and fame of that great and good man. Also
Walter, Lord Fitzwalter, the last male of the family, in 1432,
under a round arch, near the remains of his mother. An
alabaster figure of superb workmanship, laying between two
pillars on the north side of the church, represents the "Fair Matilda,"
the beautiful daughter of the second Walter Fitz-Walter, who, according
to traditionary legends, was the wife of Robin Hood; this, however, is
very apocryphal, and must be received with caution in the absence of
historical confirmation. A more probable, though more saddening, tradition which history has recorded, is that this virtuous maiden was destroyed by poison for refusing to gratify the illicit and adulterous passion
of King John. The Priory Church contains the ancient chair in which
the claimants of the Dunmow Flitch were chaired. Few who visit this
ancient church neglect to take a rest in this venerated relic of antiquity.
Some hundreds of loving hearts have sat in the old chair in amorous
juxtaposition, and many must have been the hopes and aspirations and
fond anticipations that they, at least, should live a life of happiness that

would entitle them to the Flitch, even if they failed to claim it and in the stern realities of life many must have failed to realise the hopes of their youthful days when sitting in the Bacon chair. Mr. Savill, the promoter of the modern revivals, has a *fac simile* of this chair which is kept for future presentations at Great Dunmow. History only records this old chair being used six times. Let us hope its new successor will be more in requisition. As William the Conqueror despoiled the native landowners of their broad acres, and lavished them upon his Norman lords, so did Henry VIII. despoil and suppress the monasteries of England, and grant them to his favourite courtiers. Dunmow Priory escaped the base and servile uses that some of these religious sanctuaries were subjected, and has been ever preserved for religious worship, though under a reformed faith; yet it met the common fate of all at the suppression. Its revenues were at that time valued at £173 2s. 4d. per annum, a large sum if we consider the difference in the value of money then and now. Originally the induction to this Church was by the Prior and Canons selecting one of their own body; but since the dissolution the benefice has been a *donative* or *curacy* in the gift of the Lord of the Manor of Brick-House—Major Toke,—who is patron of the benefice. The living is £72 per annum, but has been augmented with £600 of Queen Arm's Bounty, as also with £400 in two benefactions, and has been held since 1838 by the Rev. R. R. Toke, M.A., of Barnston. This ancient Church was for many years as unsightly as modern bricks and mortar could make it. Happily all has been changed by a complete restoration of the fabric, which, so far as modern improvements can go, has been transformed into a perfect shrine of beauty, and will well repay the antiquary a visit. The original "sharp-pointed stones," upon which the claimants knelt to swear, by "custom of confession," to their

"Fealty and love,"

are lost. A few years since, however, a "sharp-pointed stone" was dug up in the Churchyard with other relics. In shape it is like the pointed cut glass stopper of a decanter, and would be a stern penance for the marrow bones of the veriest quixotic enthusiast. No other stone was found to match it. It is shown to visitors as the "Bacon Stone," but its claim to that appellation is very flimsy and extremely doubtful. Mr. J. W. Savill, who has inspected all of the local churches for miles around Dunmow, has seen it, and declares it to be, to the best of his judgment, a finial or "knotte"* of one of the small "crocketted" ornaments of the old church, and of which the cathedrals of York, Salisbury and Wells, afford good specimens. The Rev. J. H. Hallett is Lord of the Manor of Little Dunmow Priory. In 1274, Roger de Saling founded a chantry in the chapel of St. Mary (the priory church), in the court of the priory, for the reception of strangers, to pray for his soul, and the souls of some other persons for ever, and endowed it with lands in Rayne.

CLAIMING THE FLITCH.

In answer to the remarks culled from "The People's History of Essex,' (see page 13 of this book) Mr. Savill states:—"In law, the wife's identity is lost in that of her husband's, therefore there would be no necessity to name her, and, from this fact alone, there is a strong inference that she was always present, or the flitch would have been granted *ex parte*.

DR. BELL'S NOTES ON DUNMOW AND SIMILAR CUSTOMS.

In Dr. Bell's work, entitled "Shakespeare's Puck and his Folk-Lore," will be found much information as to the Dunmow Flitch. The author observes, in reference to the Custom in Germany, that in a very scarce book, entitled "Curieuse Antiquitäten," published at Hamburg, in 1715, is a story called "Der Man und die Speckseite"—"The Man and the Flitch of Bacon." Further, that at Vienna, beneath the Red Tower, before it was taken down, hung a Flitch of Bacon, to which were appended these lines :—

Befind' sich irgend hir ein Mann
Der mit den Wahrheit sprecken kann,
Dass ihm sine Heurath nischt gerowe,
Und fürcht' sich nischt vor sine Frowe,
Der mag desen Backen hereunter howe;

which he interprets in similar doggerel :—

Is there to be found a married man,
That in verity declare can,
That his marriage him doth not rue,
That he has no fear of his wife for a shrew
He may this Bacon for himself down hew.

* "With crochetes on corneres with knottes of gold."

Similar stories are told in the Austrian capital of the ludicrous failures of parties who occasionally applied, such as tradition has handed down of its brother at Dunmow, or the more ancient one, perhaps, at Whichnor in Staffordshire.

"Once upon a time a man applied, and was bold enough to demand the flitch, and when a ladder was brought that he might cut down the unctuous prize, he requested that some one else would do it for him, as if he got a grease-spot on his Sunday clothes his wife would scold him terribly. Upon this the gatekeeper told him to be off ; he could have no claim to the bacon. He who fears is certainly not master at home, and has certainly rued having married."

Dr. Bell then proceeds to connect these customs with those of more remote pagan antiquity, and remarks that the custom of hanging up flitches, perhaps as a reward for fecundity in the marriage state, in imitation of the sow to which the original side belonged, is interwoven into the earliest popular antiquities of the Romans, and he cites a passage from Spence's *Polymetis* :—"Alba Longa is the place where Æneas met the white sow and thirty pigs ; and here was a very fine flitch of bacon kept in the chief temple, even in Augustus's time I find recorded in that excellent historian, Dionysius Halicarnassus."

Dr. Bell also refers to the offering of a flitch of bacon by the heathen Prussians to Percunnos, the mightiest of their triune deities, an account of which is found in Tettau and Temme's *Volkssagen*, N. 11, p. 25 :—" A mighty deity of the heathen Prussians was Percunnos. An eternal fire was kept burning before him, fed by oak billets. He was the God of thunder and fertility, and he was therefore invoked for rain and fair weather; and *in thunderstorms the flitch of bacon (speck site)* was offered to him. Even now* when it thunders the boor in Prussia takes a flitch of bacon on his shoulder, and goes with his head uncovered out of the house, and carries it into the fields, and exclaims ' O God, fall not upon my fields, and I will give thee this flitch.' When the storm is

---

*As the relation is copied from J. L. Pollonu's *De Diis Samogitiæ*, and Hartknock's *Alt und Neu Preussen*, the latter being published in 1529, it is difficult to know whether to fix this " now " at that time, or at the date of the publication of *Volkssagen*, 1837. (*Tettau.*)

passed, he takes the bacon home and consumes it with his household as a sacrifice." "Percunnos," continues Dr. Bell, "being the God of fertility, the analogy is still kept up ; and although the occasion differs, yet, when the ceremony is concluded at Dunmow, the respective couples, like the Prussian boor, will convey the Flitches to the homes rejoicing."

We have extracted Dr. Bell's notes from our friend Dr. Charnock's excellent work on "The Ancient Manorial Customs of Essex."

WHICHNOR CUSTOM.

It will not be without interest to trace the history of a Staffordshire custom similar to that of Dunmow. The Manor of Whichnor with that of Sirescote was granted by William I. to one of his Norman followers of the name of De Somerville, by the tenure of a knight's fee and three-fourths, and, like other military services, the rendering of aids and reliefs to the superior lord of the fee, which superior was the possessor of the Honour of Tutbury. Sir Philip de Somerville, a descendant of the original possessor, was a great friend and favourite of his superior lord, John of Gaunt, and his companionable qualities made him a frequent and welcome visitor to Tutbury Castle. The Duke of Lancaster, who was very remarkable for his singular and in many cases jocular institutions, wishing to free his companion from the liability of being called upon for his aid at times inconvenient to himself, established the following commutation of the moiety of his claims; that is, in all probability, for the Manor of Whichnor:—That he, Sir Philip de Somerville should find, maintain, and sustain one bacon flyke hanging in his hall at Whichnor, ready arrayed at all times of the year, except in Lent, to be given to every man or woman married, after the day and a year of their marriage be passed, and to be given to every man of religion, archbishop, prior, and to every priest after the year and day of their profession finished, or of their dignity received, in form following :—"Whensoever that any such before named will come to enquire for the bacon in their own person, or by any other for them, they shall come to the bailiff, or to the porter of the lordship of Whichnor, and shall say to them in the manner as ensueth : ' Bailiff, or Porter, I do you to know that I come for myself' (or, if he be come for another, showing for whom he demands) ' to demand one bacon flyke hanging in the hall of the Lord of Whichnor, after the form thereunto belonging.' Application being thus made, the bailiff or porter shall appoint a time for the applicant to come again, bringing with him two of his neighbours. ¯ " In the meantime, the said bailiff shall take with him twain of the freeholders of the lordship of Whichnor, and they then shall go to the Manor of Rudlow, belonging to Robert Knyghtley, and then shall summon the aforesaid Knyghtley or his bailiff commanding him to be ready at Whichnor, the day appointed, at prime of day with his carriage, that is to say, a horse and a saddle, a sack and a pryke (basket), for to convey and carry the said bacon, and come a journey out of the county of Stafford at his cost. And thus the said bailiff shall, with the said freeholders, summon all the tenants of the said manor to be ready at the day appointed, at Whichnor, for to do and perform the services which they owe to the baron. And at the day assigned all such as owe services to the baron shall be ready at the gate of the Manor of Whichnor, from the rising of the sun to noon, attending and awaiting for the coming of him that fetcheth the bacon. And when he is come there shall be delivered to him and his fellows chaplets ; and all those who shall be there to do their services due to the baron. And they shall lead the said demandant with trumpets and tabour and other manner of minstrelsy to the hall door, where he shall find the Lord of Whichnor or his steward ready to deliver the bacon in this manner: He shall inquire of him who demandeth the bacon if he has brought twain of his neighbours with him, and he must answer, They be here ready. And then the steward shall cause these two neighbours to swear, if the said demandant be a wedded man, and if, since his marriage, one year and one day be passed, and if he be a freeman or villain. And if his neighbours make oath that he hath for him all these three points rehearsed, then shall the bacon be taken down, and brought to the hall door, and there be laid upon half a quarter of wheat, and upon one other of rye. And he that

48

demandeth the bacon shall kneel upon his knee and shall hold his
right hand upon a book, which book shall be laid above the bacon and
the corn, and shall make oath in this manner:—"Hear ye, Sir Philip de
Somerville, Lord of Whichmore, mayntener and gyver of this baconne,
that I, A, sithe I wedded B, my wyfe, and sythe I hadd hyr in my kepyng
and at my wylle by a yere and a day after our marryage, I w'od not
have chaunged for none other, farer ne fowler, rycher ne pourer, ne for
none other descended of greater lyneage, slepyng ne wakyng, at noo
tyme. And yf the said B were sole, and I sole, I wolde take hyr to be
my wyfe before all the wymen in the worlde, of what condicions soever
they be, goode or evylle, so help me God and his sayntis, and thys fleshe
and all fleshes." And his neighbours shall make oath that they trust
verily he hath said truly. And if it be found by his neighbours before-
named that he be a freeman, there shall be delivered to him half a
quarter of wheat and a cheese; and if he be a villain he shall have half a
quarter of rye without cheese, and then shall Knyghtley, the Lord of
Rudlow, be called for to carry all these things before rehearsed; and the
said corn shall be laid on horse, and the bacon above it, and he to whom
the bacon appertaineth shall ascend upon his horse, and shall take the
cheese before him, if he have a horse, and if he have none the Lord of
Whichnor shall cause him to have one, and a saddle, until such time as
he has passed his lordship; and so shall they depart the Manor of Whichnor, with the corn and the bacon before him that hath won it, with
trumpets, tabrets, and other manner of minstrelsy; and all the free tenants
of Whichnor shall conduct him past the lordship of Whichnor, and
then shall all shall return except him to whom appertaineth to make the
carriage and journey out of the county of Stafford, at the cost of his Lord
of Whichnor. And if the said Robert Knyghtley do not cause the bacon
and corn to be conveyed as is rehearsed, the Lord of Whichnor shall cause
it to be carried, and shall distrain the said Robert Knyghtley for his de-
fault for one hundred shillings in his Manor of Rudlow, and shall keep
the distress so taken irrepleviable." Sir Oswald Mosley (from whose
" History of Tutbury " part of the foregoing account has that abstracted)
observes:—" The merry Sir Philip continued to treat his bacon with due

respect, for we find him granting to Hugh, son of Walter de Newbold, and Agnes, his wife, by deed, in the 16th of Edward I., several small pieces of land in Dunstall, upon condition that they should render to him and his heirs annually, eight hens at Christmas, and one chaplet or nosegay of white and red roses to decorate the bacon at Whichnor every year, on the feast of St. John the Baptist, they were also under an obligation to dress the said bacon with flowers prepared for them ten times a year, viz., to begin on Easter Eve, and continue the same monthly until the feast of St. Michael, and upon the vigil of All Saints and Christmas Eve they were to decorate the same with ivy. The Manor of Whichnor no longer remains in the family of the Somervilles. It has had various possessors, and the hall in which the flitch originally hung has been long destroyed. Leland says that Whichnor was the site of a very ancient mansion which was then in ruins, and that the spot on which it stood was subject to inundations from the Trent. Traces of the mansion are still visible in the meadows at a small distance south-west of the church. The moat is square, encompassing an acre of ground." A new building, however, has been erected, and bears the name of the Lodge, in the hall of which a piece of wood in the form of a flitch of bacon hangs near the chimney as a remembrance of the obsolete tenure.

THE CUSTOM OF DUNMOW.

By WILLIAM HARRISON AINSWORTH.

SHOWING HOW IT AROSE.

FYTTE THE FIRST.

A Fond Couple make a Vow before the Good Prior of the Convent of our Lady of Dunmow, that they have loved each other well and truly for a Twelve-month and a Day; and crave his Blessing.

I.

"What seek you here, my children dear?
Why kneel ye down thus lowly
Upon the stones, beneath the porch
Of this our Convent holy?
The Prior old the pair bespoke
In faltering speech and slowly.

II.

Their modest garb would seem proclaim
    The pair of low degree,
But though in cloth of frieze arrayed,
    A stately youth was he :—
While she, who knelt down by his side,
    Was beautiful to see.

III.

" A Twelvemonth and a Day have fled
    Since first we were united ;
And from that hour," the young man said,
    " No change our hopes has blighted.
Fond faith with fonder faith we've paid,
    And love with love requited.

IV.

" True to each other have we been ;
    No dearer object seeing,
Than each has in the other found ;
    In everything agreeing,
And every look, and word and deed
    That breed dissension fleeing.

V.

" All this we swear, and take in proof
    Our Lady of Dunmow!
For She, who sits with saints above,
    Well knows that it is so.
Attest our Vow, thou reverend man,
    And bless us, ere we go !"

VI.

The Prior old stretch'd forth his hands
    " Heaven prosper ye !" quoth he ;
" O'er such as ye, right gladly we
    Say ' *Benedicite !*'
On this, the kneeling pair uprose—
    Uprose full joyfully.

FYTTE THE SECOND.

*The Good Prior merrily bestoweth a Boon upon the Loving Couple, and
getteth a noble Recompense.*

I.

Just then, pass'd by the Convent cook—
    And moved the young man's glee;
On his broad back a mighty Flitch
    Of Bacon brown bore he
So heavy was the load. I wis,
    It scarce mote carried be.

II.

"Take ye that Flitch," the Prior cried,
  "Take it, fond pair, and go ;
Fidelity, like yours, deserves
  The boon I now bestow.
Go, feast your friends, and think upon
  The Convent of Dunmow."

III.

" Good Prior," then the youth replied,
  " Thy gift to us is dear,
Not for its worth, but that it shows
  Thou deem'st our love sincere.
And in return broad lands I give—
  Broad lands thy Convent near ;
Which shall to thee and thine produce
  A Thousand Marks a year !

IV.

" But this condition I annex,
  Or else the Grant's forsaken ;
That whensoe'er a pair shall come,
  And take the Oath we've taken,
They shall from thee and thine receive
  A goodly Flitch of Bacon.

V.

" And thus from out a simple chance
  A usage good shall grow ;
And our example of true love
  Be held up evermo :
While all who win the prize shall bless
  The Custom of Dunmow,"

VI.

" Who art thou, son," the Prior cried,
  His tones with wonder falter—
" Thou should'st not jest with reverend men,
  Nor with their feelings palter."
" I jest not, Prior, for know in me
  Sir Reginald Fitzwalter.

VII.

"I now throw off my humble garb,
  As I what I am, confest ;
The wealthiest I of wealthy men,
  Since with this treasure blest."
And as he spoke, Fitzwalter clasp'd
  His lady to his breast.

VIII.

" In peasant guise my love I won,
 Nor knew she whom she wedded ;
In peasant cot our truth we tried,
 And no disunion dreaded.
Twelve months' assurance proves our faith,
 On firmest base is steadied."

IX.

Joy reigned within those Convent walls
 When the glad news was known ;
Joy reigned within Fitzwalter's halls
 When there his bride was shown ;
No lady in the land such sweet
 Simplicity could own.
A natural grace had she, that all
 Art's graces far outshone :
Beauty and worth for want of birth
 Abundantly atone.

L'Envoy.

Hence the Custom.

What need of more? That Loving Pair
 Lived long and truly so ;
Nor ever disunited were ;—
 For one death laid them low !
And hence arose that Custom old—
 The Custom of Dunmow.

LOVE'S PROUDEST PRIZE.

By William Berry.

O Love ! thou parent of the happiest hours,
 That dawn propitious on our mortal eyes,
Whose gentlest words are frought with richest dowers
 And sweetest hopes embalmed in softest sighs !
Arise, thou Prince of Lovliness and light,
 Spread thy resplendent wings of gorgeous sheen
Before the morning rays that charm our sight,
 And with thy glorious gladness fill the scene !

Slow breaks the morn o'er Asia's hoary hills,
Till broad and bright Sol shakes his flag of flame
Touching and changing all, the orient fills
With shimmering haze a golden glow of fame!
Then lake and mountain kindle fair and far
O'er all a roseate hue of crimson light
Eclipses nature, and the morning star
Fainting with bliss pales slowly in the height!

The blushing morn that opes her am'rous arms
To woe her welcome lord with sweet embrace
In the fair freshness of her opening charms
The dull remembrance of the night to chase
Away, smiles gaily as her silent sway
From peak to plain o'er all the land extends
The opening buds expanding to her ray
Till all in one sweet perfect picture blends!

Thus o'er our lives Love spreads his splendid glow,
Till all the bleak and bare fades faint and far
In growing distance. Thus his blossoms blow
More warm and bright than Aurore's flashing car!
How sweet the mellow glow of sunny days,
Embalmed in soul-subduing light of love,
Where never tempest comes nor cloudlet strays
To dim the splendour of the blue above.

Such the felicity that blest the lot
Of two immortal in the page of fame—
Two happy souls who may not be forgot,
Whose lives Love's most peculiar care became!
He smiled in blessing on the joyous hour
In which they met. He touched each youthful heart
With his fond magic, gave them for a dower
True tenderness that never shall depart.

Taught by his art each virtue ever wears
A heavenly garb of dear attractive grace,
To them the haggard face of weary cares
Seems but to frown when they do not embrace.
One smile of Love abolishes the gloom,
One kiss, one clasp, Love reigns and sorrow flees,
The star of true affection gilds the tomb—
They live to Love, they only Love to please!

To this fond pair. the Dunmow Flitch appears
Unclaimed, a slight upon the holy spring
Of all their joys. To them the gift endears
The sacred pleasures that its teachings bring.
Thrice blest forbearance! Of domestic bliss
The happy fount, they best know how to prize,
Who long renewing the sweet peaceful kiss,
Have seen dread storms o'ershadow neighb'ring skies.

Safe in their tower of refuge they have viewed
　The howling storm with desolation spread
O'er many a bloom that steadfastly withstood
　The frosts of courtship and the youth-bloom fled.
By wisdom given, by custom conse·-rate,
　By genius dowered, by Love and peace endeared,
The ancient Flitch becomes a trophy great
　Of rarest happiness, beloved, revered.

Not this a flag from bloody fields well borne,
　Nor shield on which a conquered foeman fell,
But the bright badge of Love that knows no morn,
　Nor noon, nor night, of truth and trust proved well!
They only win this proudest prize of Love,
　Whose true affection trials never shake—
Whose trust on purest Love time's power above
　Rests surely, loving on for Love's sweet sake!

Be ours the sweet forbearance thus imprest,
　Through all the ills that fret life's daily round,
And ever faithful to the faithful breast,
　May we of Dunmow's Flitch be worthy found!

CLAIM BY A DERBYSHIRE POET.

The late John Joseph Briggs, Esquire, some time ago sent in a claim
for the Flitch, having, to the best of his belief, by matrimonial felicity
complied with the conditions of the ancient oath. In the year 1874 Mr.
and Mrs. Briggs were invited to the "Court of Hymen," holden at
Dunmow, to substantiate their application; it is, however, to be regretted,
owing to the indisposition of the former, they were unable to attend. On
the 23rd of March, 1876, Mr. Briggs died at his residence, King's Newton,
near Derby, deeply lamented by all who had the pleasure of knowing
him. He was born on the 6th of March, 1819, in the village where he
passed away. He was a landowner and farmer. From his earliest years
he was a lover of natural history, and long ago he originated in the *Field*
the column devoted to that science, and enriched the journal with most
pleasing and, at the same time, valuable contributions. It is stated, in

some years, he wrote as many as 2,500 letters, chiefly in reply to communications called forth by his papers on natural history which were inserted in various publications.

As an historical writer Mr. Briggs rendered good service by the excellent "History of Melbourne," a book issued at seven shillings and sixpence, now second-hand finds a ready market at a pound. It is a remarkable fact that 800 copies of this book were sold in three weeks, so highly was it appreciated. The work is one of great merit; it will ever remain a monument displaying his ability, industry, and serve as a model for writers of local histories.

Various were his productions on history, and kindred subjects, to the best of our publications, he contributed with his ready pen.

As a poet Mr. Briggs ranks high. In the year 1852 appeared "The Trent, and other Poems." A review in the *Critic* states,—"The book, as a poetical work, almost defies criticism. Artistically, it comes nearest Pope in balance of its sentences, and the smooth flow of the rhythm. The descriptions of the river Trent and the woods of Donnington are exceedingly truthful, but it is in his sonnets where Mr. Briggs shows his real strength. The one on 'Silence,' Wordsworth rarely, if ever, surpassed." Other reviews are equally favourable. The following is the sonnet on "Silence," which cannot fail to delight the lover of the beautiful :—

Silence hath set her finger with deep touch
Upon Creation's brow. Like a young wife, the Moon
Lifts up Night's curtains, and, with countenance mild,
Smiles on the beauteous Earth—her sleeping child.
For joy the wild flowers weep. Soft incense, such
As steals from herbs, 'midst pleasant fields in June,
Freights the night air. Each light tree's waving tress
Is edged with silver. Flocks lie motionless.
How sweet are hours spent in such scenes as this,
When Peace looks down from Heaven in plaintive mood,
And Earth, in deep tranquillity of bliss,
Becomes a suitor to fair Solitude !
What noble actions spring to fruited prime
Spring—from the seeds Thought sows in such a time !

His love of the tender sex is well expressed in the poem as follows, entitled " Woman."

It is not in seasons of sunshine and wealth,
    That we see woman's virtues shine forth ;
Nor e'en when our cheeks show the foot-prints of health,
    And joy's flowers by life's pathways have birth.

But when sickness hath sheathed in man's bosom its dart,
    Woman's nature seems all but divine :
She's the woodbine that round the scathed oak of his heart,
    Loves its delicate wreathes to entwine.

How patient her watchings—her wants then how few !—
    Man's loneliness eager to share ;
And how oft is her lily cheek bathed with the dew
    Of warm tears that hang silently there.

She heeds not the length of the cold, sunless night,
    That is robbing her cheek of its bloom;
She heeds not the taper's pale glimmering light
    That just burns through the darkness and gloom.

With an eye ever watchful—an ear that e'er hears
    Each half-uttered, each soft-whispered word,
Her vigil she keeps, and hope hushes the fears—
    The dark fears which anxiety stirred.

Oh, woman ! I love not thy beauty and grace
    (Though rich are these gifts thou dost wear) :
I love thee, because thou dost closer embrace
    Him whom sorrow hath stricken, or care.

Man may boast of fair deeds; in prowess and might,
    In arts and in arms may he shine :
But he shrinks back appalled and dismayed at a sight
    When a noble courage is thine.

With thy patient endurance he never can tend
    The lone couch where the sick one recline :
Let others choose man—boasted man—for their friend ;
    Let woman—true woman—be mine.

POEMS BY MADAME DE CHATELAIN.

Before submitting poems by Madame Clara de Chatelain, it will not
be without interest to furnish a few biographical notes. She died June
30, 1876, deeply regretted by her warm-hearted husband and many friends.
The leading English and French journals contained notices of the life of
this estimable lady at the time of her death. The memorials were col-
lected, and issued in a volume for private circulation, by Le Chevalier
de Chatelain. In the *Stratford-upon-Avon Chronicle*, of 21st July,
1876, it was kindly stated respecting Madame Clara de Chatelain :—
"This gifted lady is no more. Death, indeed, has of late been remorse-
less in taking from us bright and rare intellects. None will the
world of letters more deplore than this accomplished authoress.
We, who have known her worth, bear willing but sorrowing testi-
mony to her great merits. These columns have shewn abundant
proof in all that concerns, to use one of the titles of one of her
sweetest works, the 'True Nobility' of womanhood, she surpassingly
excelled. The wife of a man alike distinguished for literary ability,
there never was, perhaps, a union of two such opposite natures, the
husband, a Chevalier *pur sang*, with his hand ever on the hilt to dispute
the way to a foeman worthy of his steel : the wife, the very incarnation
of gentleness. Thus no small thing was it, by unanimous consent the
Dunmow Flitch was awarded to them, every condition of winning it
having been absolutely fulfilled, so for thirty years or more the tenor of
their lives was even and uninterrupted. Both alike industrious and
indefatigable, it could not here well be told how numerous, how varied,
how versatile were her works. Proud of one thing we may be, that
nationally speaking, we can claim her for our own, she having been born
n London ; but England with France shared the fruits and honours
of her labours. It pleased her usually to assume a *non de plume*, and
few of our readers but will recollect with pleasure, as they will now
sadly mourn the name and fame of 'Leopold Wray.'" We must add, on
June 1st, 1877, appeared from the Dryden Press, and issued for private
circulation, "Fleurs et Fruits : Souvenirs de feu Madame Clara de
Chatelain, née Clara de Pontigny. Dédiés a ceux qui furent et sont

H

restés nos amis. Edités par Le Chevalier de,Chatelain." It contains a
number of charming original poems in English and French, also trans-
lations. We are pleased to see announced for publication, by Mr. Basil
Pickering, 196, Piccadilly, W., the chief works in English of Madame de
Chatelain. They will include, amongst other productions, " The Statute
Fair: a Christmas Tale," " The Man of Many Daughters," the " Dale-
carlian Conjuror's Day Book." These works will be welcomed by lovers
of the beautiful in our literature.

MY CHILDHOOD'S DAYS.

In childhood's days—in childhood's days !
  The sky was pure—the grass was green,
And every flower that met our gaze,
  Through Hope's prismatic hues was seen.
How lovely then seemed every phase
  In which each season re-appears !
    What spring can vie—after years—
With childhood's days !—with childhood's days ?

In childhood's days—in childhood's days
  Our frames are weak—our hope is strong !
We bound through life's bright flowery ways,
  Wi h ringing laugh and merry song
A world of care before us lays,
  But what heed we, who know it not ?
    Our tears are brief, and soon forgot
In childhood's days !—in childhood's days.

My childhood's days—my childhood's days !
  There is magic in the word,
Half joy, half sadness, that will raise,
  So oft its welcome sound is heard.
In riper years life's rest decays,
  No laugh does e'er so jocund ring
    Nor woodland birds so sweetly sing,
Since childhood's days—since childhood's days !

My childhood's days !—my childhood's days !
  E'en while I tread life's downward hill,
Their light shines forth with weakened rays,
  That sheds a halo round me still.
And as the wearied travellers gaze
  On scenes long past looks back in vain—
    I would I might recall again—
My childhood's days !—my childhood's days.

THE LOVER'S WISHES.

A SONG OF LOVE.

This little poem—translated by my dear Clara—was written for her
(then Miss Clara de Pontigny) by myself, Chevalier de Chatelain, on the
19th January, 1843. The 13th April following, Miss de Pontigny
(the dear soul) exchanged her name for that of "Madame Clara de
Chatelain."

I would I were the cloud above,
   That screens thee from the noontide ray;
I would I were thine image, love,
   To smile on thee at dawn of day !

I would I were that flow'ret blue,
   That waves amid thine ebon hair;
Or the glass. when thou dost view
   Within its depths thy features fair.

I would—when slumbers wait on thee,
   And sweet each sense in rest enfold—
Thy guardian angel I might be,
   Who hovers round on wings of gold.

I would I were a dream that leaves
   No bitter thoughts thy peace to mar—
A dream so sweetly that deceives,
   Than duller truth 'tis better far.

I would I were a gentle dove,
   Glad tidings who to thee might bear;
To fan thee with the wings of love,
   And nestle in thy flowing hair.

I would I were the radiant spark
   Those eyes emit when day doth flee;
Nay, I would be thy shadow dark
   So I might ever follow thee.

I would I were each thing that meets
   Thine eyes where'er they rove by chance—
Each passing wish—each flower whose sweets,
   However humble, win thy glance.

I would I were the Lyre, whose chord
   Thine ear with rapt'rous shrills could bless—
I would, in one sweet word,
   I would that I were—Happiness.

This song has been set to music by Charles Cberthür, the great
harpist, and has been very well received by the public.

JOHN AND MARY; OR, A TALK ABOUT THE DUNMOW FLITCH.

By Mrs. G. M. Tweddell (Florence Cleveland), *Authoress of "Rhymes
and Sketches to Illustrate the Cleveland Dialect," etc.*

JOHN.

What think you, Mary, if we try
　To win the Dunmow Flitch?
We've lived together twenty years,
　And never had a hitch.

So smoothly we have sail'd along,
　No jerks have ever come;
We've pull'd together, as we ought,
　To make a happy home.

Your temper always is so good,
　I never knew you vary;
A loving wife you've ever been
　To me, my darling Mary.

I know I'm not so good as you,
　Although I strive to be
As good a husband to you, dear,
　As you're a wife to me.

And if we chance the prize to win,
　The merit is with you.

MARY.

Nay, nay, dear John, pray say not so!
　Them words will never do.

'Twas you who always were so good,
　. So true and kind to me;
To have the merit for myself,
　How *selfish* that would be!

Besides, it's not my due; I feel
　It all belongs to you:
You made my pathway smooth and bright,
　And ever help'd me through.

JOHN.

I have no wish to quarrel, wife,
　But now, it seems to me,
A subject has come up at last
　On which we don't agree.

It does seem strange that you and I
　At last should have a hitch;
In this one thing we can't agree,
　So we'll give up the Flitch.

Rose Cottage, Stokesley.

DUNMOW PRIORY AND FLITCH.

By GEORGE MARKHAM TWEDDELL, F.R.S.N.A., COPEN.,
Author of " Shakspere, his Times and Contemporaries,"
" The People's History of Cleveland and its Vicinage," etc., etc.

Near where the Chelmer gently winds along
Through the rich meads of Essex; country once
Of those vile Trinobantes who, in hate
Of one another, call'd the Romans in
To rule them, and resign'd their liberties,
The willing slaves of proud imperial Rome,—
Content their Mandubratius should be
The barbarous satrap of a Cæsar's throne ;
The relics of a Priory now stand,
As placid as the wheat that waves close by.

These, like all ruins, have their history ;
And, though I deem him fool who would attempt
To stop the wheels which ever onward roll
Of thy bright car, O Progress ! not less fool
Is the loud-mouth'd pretender who would claim
All wisdom for the Present Age, and thinks
The Past all ignorance and tyranny.

The Past had errors we can now avoid ;
The Present has much wrong we must redress,
Or our posterity will rank this age,
With all its light, as semi-barbarous.
Let us conserve whate'er of good we have
Received from our forefathers ; holding it
A legacy in sacred trust for those
Who will be Englishmen when we are dust.
Let us look harshly on ourselves alone ;
And, whilst we shun the errors of the Past,
Be thankful for its teachings, and thus learn
To reform the Present ; and the Future then
May thank us for our pains. As yet, we are
Far, far off from perfection, though in pride
We pipe our puny reeds in praise of all
Our little selves accomplish, and dare scorn
The parents who both made our paths and taught
Our tottering feet to walk with safety.
Wise, then, is he who neither would stand still,
As though our fathers had done all for us
That e'er should be attempted, nor would spurn
The wisdom of the Past ; but rather aim
To raise his own above all former times,

By being brave, and wise, and good himself
And cherishing those virtues in all else;
Devoutly thankful for all former good,
Whenever or wherever it appear'd,
And hopeful for the Future.
                          In such mood
Much may we learn, O Dunmow! from thy Ruins.
"Sermons in stones" they are, indeed, to those
Whose ears are open to their eloquence.
How in a place like this all human pride,
Like the soap-bubbles of our childish days,
Should burst and disappear; for pride, like them,
Is unsubstantial: would it were as pure!
      Gone were the Celt's from Dunum's pleasant brow;
No more the Romans march'd with martial pride
From Cæsaromagus; Fast Saxons too,
Though there, no longer were the conquering race,
But bow'd their necks beneath the Norman yoke,
In rightful retribution for the wrongs
They'd wrought upon the people of the land;
When Lady Juga, of the Baynard line,
Fix'd on this site to found a Priory
After the good Augustine's rule,—the monk
Whom Gregory sent, five hundred years before,
From Rome, where all was rich in monuments
Of former greatness, and still bore some share
In the world's civilization, to teach
A purer faith to Saxons, who sold slaves,
Yea, their own children, bred for guilty gain,
E'en in this isle of Britain.
                          Yonder tomb,
So chestlike in appearance, that remains
Under an arch'd recess in the south wall,
'Tis thought is hers. For near seven centuries too
The well-arm'd knight whose effigy remains,
Walter Fitz-Walter, here has " slept the sleep
That knows no waking;" his armour of proof
Pierced by the shaft of Death as easily
As his own spear pierced the poor ill-clad churl.
But most of all commend me to the tomb
Of the Fair Maud, well-known in English song,
Where she wi l live for ever, (or our bards,
From honest Michael Drayton, Shakspere's friend,
All, all must be forgot!) merry " Maid Marian,"
Wife, concubine, or call her what you will,
Of Robin Hood, England's then truest son,

Yea, England's truest king, whom she preferr'd
To the unkingly thief who stole the crown,
Murdering the rightful heir.
                                        Fair was her form
As alabaster, doubt not; it is well
The alabaster here should mark the grave
Wherein repose her ashes; but she lives,
Ay, and shall live for aye, in English hearts,
Or they shall cease to heave responsive thrills
To our unequall'd ballads: and Sydney says,
(Noble Sir Philip, flower of chivalry,)
He never heard the song of Chevy Chase,
Even though it were " by some blind crowder " sung,
With voice as rough as e'er the style was rude,
Without finding his heart (O, what a heart!)
" Moved more than with a trump-t."
                                        Robin Hood!
The ballads English songsters long have sung
Of thee and of thy woodcraft; how thou plagued
The plaguers of thy country; how thou robb'd
The robbers of thy England. and bestow'd
The plunder of the plunderers on the poor.
These moved men's hearts for ages: when they cease
To move our children, may those children sleep
As still in death as Marian's effigy
In alabaster on yon ancient tomb!
    I would not, if I could, recall the Past;
Unless 'twere for a day or two, to show
Better than tongue or pen can ever do,
What was the real condition of our isle,
In palace, castle, monastery, and cot,
In our forefathers' days.
                                        And yet I love
All innocent enjoyments for their sakes;
And good Old Customs are to me as bonds
To bind us in a loving brotherhood,
Though passing through the grave. And thine, Dunmow!
That gave a Flitch of Bacon to the Wife
And Husband who could swear they ne'er had rued,
E'en for a moment, that they plighted troth;
That, for a twelvemonth and a day at least,
They never once had done an unkind thing,
They never once had spoken unkind word,
They ne'er had harbour'd unkind thought at all
Of one another; but had lived and loved
With that delightful harmony of soul

All married couples always ought to do ;
Thine was a Custom, Dunmow, that I love,—
And honour to our Ainsworth. Andrews, both,
For daring to restore it.
                                        Keep it up,
In peaceful, sober jollity, for aye.
Neither too loose, like Charles's Cavaliers,
Nor primly prudish like those Puritans
(The sourest of their tribe) who seem'd to think
Life's pilgrimage should be a purgatory,
And look'd on earth—this glorious work of God,
Who sends us flowers to blow, and birds to sing,
And tints each ever-changing cloud with beauty,—
Yet, seen through jaundiced eyes, was spurn'd by them
As though it were a hell.
                                        Courage, my friends !
Our ancestors were wise to mix delights
With needful labours ; they were not such slaves
As some have thought them, taken as a whole.
Their pride of caste did not far separate
The vassal from his lord. And they did well
To mix in merriment, as oft they fought,
Shoulder to shoulder. And the Dunmow Flitch
Is only low and vulgar to the herd
Of crawling creatures who gave hands, not hearts—
Mere legal prostitution—to gain gold,
Or lands, position, title, not to love
With that true love which melts two hearts to one ;
Love that can make true marriage in the sight
Of Heaven, though it be under Sherwood's oaks,
Without e'en Friar Tuck ; love, without which
The solemn rite beneath cathedral domes
Is perjury to God.
                                        Such are the thoughts,
O Dunmow, that thy Flitch (once more revived,
According to the Custom of our sires)
Calls up within my soul. Let it be
A yearly Custom, and pollute it not
With drunkenness, riot, or gluttony ;
But keep it pure as Chastity herself
Could wish to see it ; worthy of this isle
We glory in as dear old Anglo-land,
The abode of Honour, Purity, and Love.

Rose Cottage, Stokesley.

Printed at the " Eastern Morning News " Office, 42, Whitefriargate, Hull.

www.ingramcontent.com/pod-product-compliance
Lightning Source LLC
Chambersburg PA
CBHW021533270326
41930CB00008B/1223